THE ONE TRUE GOSPEL

Galatians 1:1–10

GETTING STARTED

Since the beginning of Christianity, people have tried to redefine the message of the gospel and what it means. In your own words, how would you define the gospel?

SETTING THE STAGE

Even in the days of the early church, believers in Christ struggled to find agreement on what is the "gospel." Is it simply that Jesus gave His own life on the cross so we might be set free from our sins and experience eternal life with Him? Or does the gospel require something more—such as our ability to follow a set of rules and regulations on how to live?

This is the debate Paul confronted as he composed his letter to the Galatians. After he had planted the church in Galatia on one of his missionary journeys, he learned that certain Jewish Christians from Jerusalem (known as the "Judaizers") had arrived and were trying to convince the new believers their faith wasn't complete unless it was accompanied by obedience to the rituals and requirements of the Old Testament. The Judaizers taught that in order to be saved, a follower of Jesus had to *live as a Jew*. This message posed a real threat to the new church. It seemed the gospel—the *good news that salvation is a gift*—wasn't as good or as simple as the Galatian Christians had been led to believe.

In response to this, Paul preached that Jesus alone saves. He held that the additional requirements of the Judaizers, such as circumcision, were not needed for salvation. No one can justify himself or herself before God—it is only in Christ that anyone is justified. This is the incredible reality of the gospel. We cannot save ourselves by any effort whatsoever. Our only hope is grace and grace alone. And when we place our trust in Jesus, we are saved!

EXPLORING THE TEXT

Greeting (Galatians 1:1–5)

---

[1] Paul, an apostle (not from men nor through man, but through Jesus Christ and God the Father who raised Him from the dead), [2] and all the brethren who are with me,

To the churches of Galatia:

JEREMIAH
BIBLE STUDY SERIES

GALATIANS

THE PATH TO FREEDOM

DR. DAVID JEREMIAH

Prepared by Peachtree Publishing Services

HarperChristian
Resources

GALATIANS
JEREMIAH BIBLE STUDY SERIES

© 2019 by Dr. David Jeremiah

Requests for information should be addressed to:
HarperChristian Resources, 3900 Sparks Dr. SE, Grand Rapids, Michigan 49546

ISBN 978-0-310-09166-0 (softcover)
ISBN 978-0-310-09167-7 (ebook)

Published in Nashville, Tennessee, by Thomas Nelson. Thomas Nelson is a registered trademark of HarperCollins Christian Publishing, Inc.

Produced with assistance of Peachtree Publishing Service (www.PeachtreePublishingServices.com). Project staff include Christopher D. Hudson, Randy Southern, and Peter Blankenship.

All Scripture quotations are taken from The Holy Bible, New King James Version. Copyright © 1979, 1980, 1982 by Thomas Nelson. All rights reserved.

HarperChristian Resources titles may be purchased in bulk for church, business, fundraising, or ministry use. For information, please e-mail ResourceSpecialist@ChurchSource.com.

First Printing November 2019 / Printed in the United States of America
24 25 26 27 28 LBC 10 9 8 7 6

CONTENTS

INTRODUCTION TO
The Letter to the Galatians

"Stand fast therefore in the liberty by which Christ has made us free, and do not be entangled again with a yoke of bondage" (Galatians 5:1). The issue of slavery versus freedom lies at the heart of the letter to the Galatians. In this case, *freedom* is represented by faith—faith in God's grace and in Jesus' sacrifice. *Slavery* is represented by the Law of Moses—the system of trying to live up to the regulations in the Old Testament covenant that God had given to Moses at Mount Sinai. The Galatian believers had been given freedom when they put their faith in Christ, but they had turned their backs on that freedom and were again embracing the law as a means of salvation. They were convinced they still needed to obey endless rules and rituals to make themselves acceptable to God. But the message of this letter is that God's grace cannot be earned—for if it could, it would not be grace.

AUTHOR AND DATE

The writer of this letter identifies himself as the apostle Paul (see 1:1), and he offers convincing biographical details throughout the letter to support his authorship. The events he discusses align with accounts about his life given in the book of Acts and other epistles, and the theology aligns with Paul's teachings in his other letters. Only the more mechanical aspects of authorship are debated today, such as why Paul writes toward the end of the letter, "See with what large letters I have written to you with my own hand" (6:11). Most likely, this indicates the letter was recorded by a scribe on Paul's behalf, with the apostle picking up the pen here and there to authenticate that the message is from him. Paul is believed to have composed the letter either in AD 48 (if the term *Galatians* refers to churches Paul founded during his first missionary journey) or in AD 52 (if the term refers to churches he founded in the region during his second journey).

BACKGROUND AND SETTING

Paul's letter to the Galatians offers a snapshot into a battle for their souls. Paul had led the Galatians to Christ on one of his previous missionary journeys. He had introduced them to God's grace and salvation and rejoiced when they embraced the new faith. But when certain leaders of the church in Jerusalem (called the Judaizers) heard what was happening, they sent emissaries to Galatia to infiltrate the church and convince the members they needed to incorporate the Old Testament law into their faith. These emissaries persuaded the Galatians to believe that in addition to faith in Christ, they had to be circumcised and submit to the Law of Moses. When Paul learned what these emissaries were doing, he sent this letter to refute their claims and to remind the Galatians of the freedom they had experienced in Christ.

KEY THEMES

Several key themes are prominent in the letter to the Galatians. The first is the *nature of Paul's authority*. The Judaizers, in an effort to bolster their own claims, had challenged Paul's authority in bringing the "gospel of grace" to the Galatians and were undermining his legitimacy as an apostle. In response, Paul recounted the circumstances of his conversion—and how he had gone from persecuting Christians to being persecuted for his own Christian faith (see 1:6–10). He told them, in no uncertain terms, that his gospel message was the one true gospel—the same as that of Peter, John, and James, the other "pillars" of the Jerusalem church.

A second theme is that *justification comes through faith alone*. The Jewish leaders who had come from the Jerusalem church were challenging this key tenet of Christianity, convincing the Galatian believers that faith was only the *beginning* of salvation. These Judaizers claimed that in order to gain God's favor, the Galatian believers also had to submit to circumcision and keep the Law of Moses. But the apostle Paul insisted that the only way a person can be made right with God is by faith in Jesus Christ (see 2:15–16).

Paul spends so much of the letter countering their elevation of the law that it becomes a third theme in the book: *the law was designed to help people come to grips with their inability to follow it*. The teachers from Jerusalem had evidently raised the question that if salvation came through faith in Christ alone—as the apostle Paul was professing—the law ultimately served no purpose. Paul was clear in his rebuttal that the law had been given to display our sinfulness and drive us to Christ (see 3:19–25).

A fourth theme is *how Christians should live out the freedom God has given them*. Paul needed to address not only those individuals who were ascribing to the idea they could "earn" their salvation by following the law but also those who were succumbing to a form of hedonism by misunderstanding God's grace. These individuals were reasoning that because Jesus' sacrifice was all that was required for salvation, they were free to do anything they liked. Paul recast the issue for the Galatians and helped them see that true Christian freedom expresses itself in acts of loving service (see 5:7–15). God's grace should naturally motivate them to love Him, walk in the Spirit, and seek to do good works for their neighbors.

KEY APPLICATIONS

Galatians is a powerful and practical book. In this letter, Paul shows us that faith in the Lord Jesus Christ is enough to make us right with God. He urges each of us to stand firm in the freedom Christ has given us. And he encourages us that living an abundant Christian life is possible as we walk in the Spirit.

³ Grace to you and peace from God the Father and our Lord Jesus Christ, ⁴ who gave Himself for our sins, that He might deliver us from this present evil age, according to the will of our God and Father, ⁵ to whom be glory forever and ever. Amen.

---

1. Paul was under attack by certain leaders in the Jerusalem church who were questioning his authority and the validity of the message he had preached. Given this, what is significant about the way Paul describes his apostleship (see verse 1)?

_____

_____

_____

_____

_____

_____

_____

2. How did Paul define the *gospel* (see verses 4–5)? How does Paul's definition compare with your own?

_____

_____

_____

_____

_____

_____

_____

_____

Only One Gospel (Galatians 1:6–10)

⁶ I marvel that you are turning away so soon from Him who called you in the grace of Christ, to a different gospel, ⁷ which is not another; but there are some who trouble you and want to pervert the gospel of Christ. ⁸ But even if we, or an angel from heaven, preach any other gospel to you than what we have preached to you, let him be accursed. ⁹ As we have said before, so now I say again, if anyone preaches any other gospel to you than what you have received, let him be accursed.

¹⁰ For do I now persuade men, or God? Or do I seek to please men? For if I still pleased men, I would not be a bondservant of Christ.

3. What was the source of Paul's *marveling* or *astonishment* as it related to the believers in Galatia (see verses 6–7)?

_____

_____

_____

_____

_____

4. The word Paul used for *accursed* is the translation of the Greek word *anathema*, which means "to be set aside to God for destruction." According to Paul, who are those who are accursed (see verses 8–9)? Why does Paul use such strong language?

_____

_____

_____

_____

_____

GOING DEEPER

Paul omits his typical "thanksgiving" section—where he praises God for the faithfulness of the church—in his letter to the Galatians. This points to the urgency he felt in calling out the error of the Judaizers. This was not the first time God's people had been forced to deal with false teachers. In the following passage, Moses—the giver of the Law—offered the following guidance to the Israelites on how to identify a false prophet.

Identifying a False Prophet (Deuteronomy 18:15–22)

15 "The LORD your God will raise up for you a Prophet like me from your midst, from your brethren. Him you shall hear, 16 according to all you desired of the LORD your God in Horeb in the day of the assembly, saying, 'Let me not hear again the voice of the LORD my God, nor let me see this great fire anymore, lest I die.'

17 "And the LORD said to me: 'What they have spoken is good. 18 I will raise up for them a Prophet like you from among their brethren, and will put My words in His mouth, and He shall speak to them all that I command Him. 19 And it shall be that whoever will not hear My words, which He speaks in My name, I will require it of him. 20 But the prophet who presumes to speak a word in My name, which I have not commanded him to speak, or who speaks in the name of other gods, that prophet shall die.' 21 And if you say in your heart, 'How shall we know the word which the LORD has not spoken?'—22 when a prophet speaks in the name of the LORD, if the thing does not happen or come to pass, that is the thing which the LORD has not spoken; the prophet has spoken it presumptuously; you shall not be afraid of him.

5. The Israelites were about to enter a land filled with pagan ideology. For this reason, the Lord needed to clarify how they could discern a true prophet from a false one. Why did God first specify the importance of following the instruction of a prophet who was truly from Him? What were the penalties for failing to do this (see verses 15–19)?

_____

_____

_____

_____

_____

_____

_____

6. What guidelines did God provide for how to distinguish a false prophet from a true one (see verses 20–22)? How does this help explain why it was critical for Paul to show the believers in Galatia that he was a true "prophet" from God who had brought them the true gospel of Christ?

_____

_____

_____

_____

_____

_____

_____

_____

_____

Paul was not the only apostle in the early church who had to deal with the problem of false teachers infiltrating the body of Christ. In the following passage, the disciple John—much like Moses before him—gives his readers some advice on how to distinguish the true prophets of God from the false teachers who had crept into their congregations.

Testing the Spirits (1 John 4:1–6)

[1] Beloved, do not believe every spirit, but test the spirits, whether they are of God; because many false prophets have gone out into the world. [2] By this you know the Spirit of God: Every spirit that confesses that Jesus Christ has come in the flesh is of God, [3] and every spirit that does not confess that Jesus Christ has come in the flesh is not of God. And this is the spirit of the Antichrist, which you have heard was coming, and is now already in the world.

[4] You are of God, little children, and have overcome them, because He who is in you is greater than he who is in the world. [5] They are of the world. Therefore they speak as of the world, and the world hears them. [6] We are of God. He who knows God hears us; he who is not of God does not hear us. By this we know the spirit of truth and the spirit of error.

7. What does John mean when he tells the believers to "test the spirits" to see whether they are of God (see verse 1)? What is the purpose of doing this?

8. What are the traits of a true prophet? What are the traits of a false prophet (see verses 2–5)? How does being "of God" help us to distinguish between the two?

_____

_____

_____

_____

_____

_____

_____

_____

_____

_____

_____

_____

_____

_____

_____

REVIEWING THE STORY

The apostle Paul begins his letter by calling out the believers in Galatia who had deserted the true gospel in favor of one that was based on works. The Judaizers were teaching that salvation is dependent on both the work of Christ _and_ on a person's ability to adhere to the rules and regulations of the Jewish law. But Paul makes it clear that he and these Judaizers are at odds. His message to the Christians of Galatia is that there is _one_ God, _one_ Savior, _one_ gospel, and _one_ way of salvation. Believers are not justified because they obey the law—they are justified solely on the basis of their faith in Jesus.

9. What two points did Paul emphasize in his greeting to the Galatians (see Galatians 1:3)?

_____

_____

_____

_____

_____

_____

_____

10. What did Jesus accomplish on the cross by dying for our sins (see Galatians 1:4)?

_____

_____

_____

_____

_____

_____

_____

11. How did Paul describe the work of the Judaizers from Jerusalem (see Galatians 1:7)?

_____

_____

_____

_____

_____

_____

12. Why was Paul so passionate about getting the meaning of the gospel right? Is the meaning of the gospel as important to you? Explain.

APPLYING THE MESSAGE

13. Why do think a gospel based on works—rather than faith in Christ alone—would be compelling to certain people? When are times in your life that you have been tempted to ascribe to such a gospel of law and works?

14. The word *gospel* means "good news." According to this lesson, why is the true gospel *good news* for every person—sinner and saint alike? What are some ways you can remind yourself (and others) of the importance and significance of the gospel each day?

REFLECTING ON THE MEANING

For Paul, the nature and content of the message of the gospel of grace was of utmost importance. In the first two chapters of this letter, the word *gospel* is found ten times! After his usual greeting of grace and peace, Paul's opening words to the Galatians set forth three major truths about Christ's death that we must never forget.

First, the death of Christ was *voluntary*. Christ "gave Himself," for our sins. No one made Jesus go to the cross. He did it Himself—of His own free will. The first thing to remember about the gospel is the voluntary death of Christ on the cross.

Second, the death of Christ was *vicarious*. The word *vicarious* means to do something on behalf of another person—in other words, to do something in someone else's place. Paul says that Christ died for "our sins." He went to the cross where we deserved to go. He died in the place where we deserved to die. He paid the penalty for our sins in our place. He was our vicarious substitute on the cross.

Third, the death of Christ was *victorious*. Paul writes in Galatians 1:4 that Christ died that "He might deliver us from this present evil age, according to the will of our God and Father." The word *deliver* suggests that Christ has conducted a successful rescue operation and set us free from the one who held us captive. He rescued us from this present evil age.

Since Christ has done all of this—voluntarily giving Himself for us, taking our place in death, rescuing us out of this age—how presumptuous we must seem to Him when we try to add something human to that which He has already done! It was this very thing that so angered Paul. The believers in the Gentile churches were being taught that what Jesus did through his death on the cross wasn't enough. It may have been adequate for their initial salvation, but their continued salvation depended on their own performance of good works. Paul challenges this dangerous idea consistently throughout his letter.

So what is the gospel? Simply this—Christ died, Christ was buried, and Christ rose again. His death was on our behalf as the Son of God.

That is the pure gospel of the grace of God. It is not a matter of law *and* grace—it is a matter of law *or* grace. It is grace and grace alone!

JOURNALING YOUR RESPONSE

What are some ways you are tempted to base your relationship with God on your performance? How would your relationship with God be different if you based it solely on His grace?

GRACE UNDER FIRE

Galatians 1:11–24

GETTING STARTED

The apostle Paul had an encounter with Jesus on the road to Damascus that forever changed his life—and the course of human history. What is the most unforgettable encounter with the grace of Jesus that you or a loved one has experienced?

_____

_____

_____

_____

_____

_____

_____

_____

_____

_____

_____

_____

_____

_____

SETTING THE STAGE

As we have seen, the Judaizers believed Paul was in error by not requiring his Gentile converts to practice the laws of Judaism. After all, they had come from a Jewish background—and they naturally assumed those rules and regulations were a component of the Christian faith. Many even questioned Paul's motives and implied that he was trying to make Christianity easy on the Gentiles to win their favor.

Paul refutes these allegations in this next section of his letter by making it clear that being liked or popular is not his priority. After reminding the Galatian believers that he has taught them the *true* gospel, he writes, "For do I now persuade men, or God? Or do I seek to please men? For if I still pleased men, I would not be a bondservant of Christ" (1:10). Here the apostle makes it very clear that as a servant of Jesus Christ, his only desire in communicating the message of free grace is to please God.

Paul did not create the gospel he was proclaiming, nor was he taught it by other humans. Rather, to his amazement, "it came through the revelation of Jesus Christ" (verse 12). God had revealed His Son to Paul—an ultra-orthodox Jew—that he might tell the Gentile nations the God of Israel loved them as much as He loved Israel! It was a straightforward message from the heart of God . . . a gospel Paul could never have fabricated.

EXPLORING THE TEXT

Paul's Call to Apostleship (Galatians 1:11–17)

---

¹¹ But I make known to you, brethren, that the gospel which was preached by me is not according to man. ¹² For I neither received it from man, nor was I taught it, but it came through the revelation of Jesus Christ.

¹³ For you have heard of my former conduct in Judaism, how I persecuted the church of God beyond measure and tried to destroy it. ¹⁴ And I advanced in Judaism beyond many of my contemporaries

in my own nation, being more exceedingly zealous for the traditions of my fathers.

¹⁵ But when it pleased God, who separated me from my mother's womb and called me through His grace, ¹⁶ to reveal His Son in me, that I might preach Him among the Gentiles, I did not immediately confer with flesh and blood, ¹⁷ nor did I go up to Jerusalem to those who were apostles before me; but I went to Arabia, and returned again to Damascus.

---

1. Paul gives his testimony in these verses so he can make the point that he is the most unlikely person to ever have trumped-up a gospel according to grace (see verses 13–14). What was Paul like before he became a Christian?

_____

_____

_____

_____

2. What did Paul say happened to him at the time of his conversion (see verses 15–16)?

_____

_____

_____

_____

_____

Paul's Visit to Jerusalem (Galatians 1:18–24)

¹⁸ Then after three years I went up to Jerusalem to see Peter, and remained with him fifteen days. ¹⁹ But I saw none of the other apostles

except James, the Lord's brother. [20](Now concerning the things which I write to you, indeed, before God, I do not lie.)

[21]Afterward I went into the regions of Syria and Cilicia. [22]And I was unknown by face to the churches of Judea which were in Christ. [23]But they were hearing only, "He who formerly persecuted us now preaches the faith which he once tried to destroy." [24]And they glorified God in me.

---

3. In Paul's day, the term *Arabia* (see verse 17) referred to an area that extended from the Red Sea in the south to the Euphrates River in the north. What might be some reasons why Paul chose to go away by himself and remain somewhat isolated for three years?

_____

_____

_____

_____

_____

4. Why do you think Paul stresses that he only met with Peter and James while he was in Jerusalem (see verses 18–20)? How is Paul using all of these biographical details to support his claim that the gospel he has preached came directly to him from God?

_____

_____

_____

_____

_____

GOING DEEPER

Paul first appears in the Bible at the stoning of Stephen—a believer who was put to death at the hands of the Jewish religious leaders for "blaspheming" the Lord (see Acts 7:57–60). Paul (at that time known as Saul) consented to his death and then made "havoc of the church, entering every house, and dragging off men and women, committing them to prison" (8:3). However, as the following account relates, something miraculous happened to Paul that forever changed his life when he set off to persecute believers in the city of Damascus.

Paul Meets the Risen Christ (Acts 9:1–9)

¹ Then Saul, still breathing threats and murder against the disciples of the Lord, went to the high priest ² and asked letters from him to the synagogues of Damascus, so that if he found any who were of the Way, whether men or women, he might bring them bound to Jerusalem.

³ As he journeyed he came near Damascus, and suddenly a light shone around him from heaven. ⁴ Then he fell to the ground, and heard a voice saying to him, "Saul, Saul, why are you persecuting Me?"

⁵ And he said, "Who are You, Lord?"

Then the Lord said, "I am Jesus, whom you are persecuting. It is hard for you to kick against the goads."

⁶ So he, trembling and astonished, said, "Lord, what do You want me to do?"

Then the Lord said to him, "Arise and go into the city, and you will be told what you must do."

⁷ And the men who journeyed with him stood speechless, hearing a voice but seeing no one. ⁸ Then Saul arose from the ground, and when his eyes were opened he saw no one. But they led him by the hand and brought him into Damascus. ⁹ And he was three days without sight, and neither ate nor drank.

5. Paul was a zealous Pharisee who thought he was doing God's will by eliminating those who claimed Jesus had risen from the dead and was the Son of God. How did God get Paul's attention and reveal the error in his thinking?

_____

_____

_____

_____

6. What might be some reasons why God chose to strike Paul with blindness (see verses 7–8)?

_____

_____

_____

_____

_____

Ananias Baptizes Paul (Acts 9:10–18)

[10] Now there was a certain disciple at Damascus named Ananias; and to him the Lord said in a vision, "Ananias."

And he said, "Here I am, Lord."

[11] So the Lord said to him, "Arise and go to the street called Straight, and inquire at the house of Judas for one called Saul of Tarsus, for behold, he is praying. [12] And in a vision he has seen a man named Ananias coming in and putting his hand on him, so that he might receive his sight."

[13] Then Ananias answered, "Lord, I have heard from many about this man, how much harm he has done to Your saints in Jerusalem. [14] And here he has authority from the chief priests to bind all who call on Your name."

¹⁵ But the Lord said to him, "Go, for he is a chosen vessel of Mine to bear My name before Gentiles, kings, and the children of Israel. ¹⁶ For I will show him how many things he must suffer for My name's sake."

¹⁷ And Ananias went his way and entered the house; and laying his hands on him he said, "Brother Saul, the Lord Jesus, who appeared to you on the road as you came, has sent me that you may receive your sight and be filled with the Holy Spirit." ¹⁸ Immediately there fell from his eyes something like scales, and he received his sight at once; and he arose and was baptized.

---

7. Why was Ananias afraid to meet with Paul (see verses 10–14)? How does this support Paul's claim that he had "persecuted the church of God beyond measure" (Galatians 1:13)?

_____

_____

_____

_____

_____

_____

8. What did God say was Paul's mission in the world (see Acts 9:15–16)? How was Paul carrying out this mission (see Galatians 1:23–24)?

_____

_____

_____

_____

_____

_____

REVIEWING THE STORY

In this section of the letter, Paul detailed two reasons why the Galatian believers could trust his gospel. First, Paul described the *basis* of his message. He emphasized the gospel he preached did not come from a human source or from human motivations. Instead, it was revealed to him directly by Christ. Second, Paul reminded the Galatians of the *background* to his message. Before his conversion, he attempted to destroy the Christian church. But after he was saved, he retreated to Arabia for three years of solitude before eventually making the trip to Jerusalem, where he spent fifteen days with Peter. From there, he traveled to Syria and Cilicia, where people knew of his former reputation and rejoiced in the transformation they saw in him.

9. What was unique about the gospel that the apostle Paul preached (see Galatians 1:11–12)?

_____

_____

_____

_____

10. Why do you think Paul did not meet with anyone but went straight into Arabia immediately after his conversion (see Galatians 1:15–17)?

_____

_____

_____

_____

11. What did Paul do when he finally made the trip to Jerusalem (see Galatians 1:18–19)?

_____

_____

_____

_____

12. How did the churches that were in Judea respond when they heard about Paul's preaching? How do you think that helped Paul (see Galatians 1:21–24)?

_____

_____

_____

_____

APPLYING THE MESSAGE

13. In Galatians 1:15, Paul says the gospel message finally penetrated his heart "when it pleased God." How can you find hope in those words as you pray for loved ones who have rejected the gospel message?

_____

_____

_____

14. What have you found to be the best strategy for dealing with someone who is vehemently opposed to Jesus?

_____

_____

_____

REFLECTING ON THE MEANING

Paul ended his description of the events surrounding his conversion by saying he had some influence in Judea. As he states, "I was unknown by face to the churches in Judea which were in Christ. But they were hearing only, 'He who formerly persecuted us now preaches the faith which he once tried to destroy.' And they glorified God in me" (Galatians 1:22–24).

Paul wasn't influential because of anything he had done himself. He was influential because of what God, in His grace, had done in him. Notice the last phrase in verse 24: "And they glorified God in me." In other words, when the churches in Judea saw what had happened to Paul, they didn't praise him—they praised God for His amazing grace and power.

Likewise, when we look at our own lives and see the remarkable results of God's grace at work, we should be compelled to give God all the glory and honor. Jesus put it best when He said in Matthew 5:16, "Let your light so shine before men, that they may see your good works and glorify your Father in heaven."

JOURNALING YOUR RESPONSE

What changes have people noticed in you since you encountered Jesus?

THE FREEDOM FIGHTER

Galatians 2:1–10

GETTING STARTED

Paul faced a great deal of criticism as it related to his authority and the message he was preaching. When is a time you faced similar criticism? How did you respond?

_____

_____

_____

_____

_____

_____

_____

_____

_____

_____

_____

SETTING THE STAGE

After Paul's conversion to Christ and his sojourn in Arabia, he began a series of missionary journeys to plant churches in the Gentile world.

On one of these journeys, he founded a series of churches in the Roman province of Galatia, preaching to them the message that salvation comes through faith in Christ alone. As we have seen, he defended this message when the Judaizers called his authority and teaching into question. Now, in this next section of Galatians, Paul continues to defend himself against the accusations of the false teachers from Jerusalem. Bondage and control are tenacious things. Those who have control over you will do almost anything to keep you in bondage.

As you read the letter of Galatians and compare it to passages in Acts, it becomes clear that one of the great concerns of the would-be leaders from Jerusalem was they were losing control. The grace of God was setting people free, and the Judaizers knew they would no longer be able to manipulate them. And since Paul was the great freedom fighter who preached the gospel of grace, he became their archenemy. So when the Judaizers could find no way to attack his *message*, they attacked *him*. Their basic claim was that Paul couldn't be from God because his gospel was completely different from the one preached by the pillars of the Jerusalem church—Peter, James, and John.

As Paul discovered, the enemies of the gospel are shrewd. They are motivated and energized by Satan himself . . . and Satan does not give up easily. If we block him at one point, he will change his attack and may even use a strategy that is in direct contrast to his original one. This is why Paul felt such a need to defend himself and counter the Judaizers' accusation. He did so by pointing out that he and the rest of the apostles received the *same* gospel from the Lord. It wasn't the apostles' gospel, and it wasn't his gospel—it was the *Lord's* gospel.

EXPLORING THE TEXT

Defending the Gospel (Galatians 2:1–5)

[1] Then after fourteen years I went up again to Jerusalem with Barnabas, and also took Titus with me. [2] And I went up by revelation,

and communicated to them that gospel which I preach among the Gentiles, but privately to those who were of reputation, lest by any means I might run, or had run, in vain. ³ Yet not even Titus who was with me, being a Greek, was compelled to be circumcised. ⁴ And this occurred because of false brethren secretly brought in (who came in by stealth to spy out our liberty which we have in Christ Jesus, that they might bring us into bondage), ⁵ to whom we did not yield submission even for an hour, that the truth of the gospel might continue with you.

---

1. Whom did Paul take with him on his visit to Jerusalem? What did Paul say was the purpose of this visit (see verse 2)?

_____

_____

_____

_____

_____

_____

2. Paul notes that while he was with the elders in Jerusalem, there were some who called for Titus, his Gentile coworker, to be circumcised in accordance with Jewish law. How does Paul use this event to show his readers that the apostles in Jerusalem supported him and his message (see verses 3–5)? Why did Paul feel the need to stress this point?

_____

_____

_____

_____

_____

_____

Defending the Gospel (Galatians 2:6–10)

⁶ But from those who seemed to be something—whatever they were, it makes no difference to me; God shows personal favoritism to no man—for those who seemed to be something added nothing to me. ⁷ But on the contrary, when they saw that the gospel for the uncircumcised had been committed to me, as the gospel for the circumcised was to Peter ⁸ (for He who worked effectively in Peter for the apostleship to the circumcised also worked effectively in me toward the Gentiles), ⁹ and when James, Cephas, and John, who seemed to be pillars, perceived the grace that had been given to me, they gave me and Barnabas the right hand of fellowship, that we should go to the Gentiles and they to the circumcised. ¹⁰ They desired only that we should remember the poor, the very thing which I also was eager to do.

3. Paul's critics had questioned his authority to deliver the gospel he was preaching to the Gentiles. How does Paul show that "those who seemed to be something" (meaning those who had status in the Jerusalem church) did not try to alter his message (see verse 6–9)?

_____

_____

_____

_____

_____

_____

_____

_____

_____

_____

4. How does Paul describe the difference between his mission and Peter's mission as it relates to the gospel? How did the church support both missions (see verses 7–9)?

_____

_____

_____

_____

_____

_____

GOING DEEPER

Paul writes that when he visited the elders of the church in Jerusalem, "not even Titus who was with me, being a Greek, was compelled to be circumcised" (2:3). The practice of circumcision, a tangible sign of God's covenant with His people in the Old Testament, was one of the key issues that drove the Judaizers. The following account reveals how God first established the practice with Abraham, the patriarch of the Jewish people, and His reasons for implementing it.

The Sign of the Covenant (Genesis 17:9–14)

⁹ And God said to Abraham: "As for you, you shall keep My covenant, you and your descendants after you throughout their generations. ¹⁰ This is My covenant which you shall keep, between Me and you and your descendants after you: Every male child among you shall be circumcised; ¹¹ and you shall be circumcised in the flesh of your foreskins, and it shall be a sign of the covenant between Me and you. ¹² He who is eight days old among you shall be circumcised, every male child in your generations, he who is born in your house or bought with money from any foreigner who is not your descendant. ¹³ He who is born in your house and he who is bought with your money

must be circumcised, and My covenant shall be in your flesh for an everlasting covenant. ¹⁴ And the uncircumcised male child, who is not circumcised in the flesh of his foreskin, that person shall be cut off from his people; he has broken My covenant."

---

5. The meaning of the word *covenant* in the Old Testament typically refers to a bond between two or more parties. In this case, the bond was between God and Abraham—and each party had certain obligations to fulfill. What did God require of Abraham to show that he was willing to enter into the obligations of the covenant (see verses 10–11)?

6. The practice of circumcision was a sign that a person had decided to follow God and agree to the terms of the covenant. Given this, why was this practice such an important part of Jewish faith? Why did the Judaizers emphasize this same practice for Christians as well?

The issue of circumcision—and the larger question it represented as to whether Gentile believers needed to adopt Jewish practices to be considered Christians—was a major point of contention in the early church. In the following passage, Luke relates how the matter was finally decided by the church in Jerusalem and the decision regarding the Gentiles that was reached.

The Jerusalem Decree (Acts 15:22–29)

[22] Then it pleased the apostles and elders, with the whole church, to send chosen men of their own company to Antioch with Paul and Barnabas, namely, Judas who was also named Barsabas, and Silas, leading men among the brethren.

[23] They wrote this letter by them:

The apostles, the elders, and the brethren,

To the brethren who are of the Gentiles in Antioch, Syria, and Cilicia:

Greetings.

[24] Since we have heard that some who went out from us have troubled you with words, unsettling your souls, saying, "You must be circumcised and keep the law"—to whom we gave no such commandment—[25] it seemed good to us, being assembled with one accord, to send chosen men to you with our beloved Barnabas and Paul, [26] men who have risked their lives for the name of our Lord Jesus Christ. [27] We have therefore sent Judas and Silas, who will also report the same things by word of mouth. [28] For it seemed good to the Holy Spirit, and to us, to lay upon you no greater burden than these necessary things: [29] that you abstain from things offered to idols, from blood, from things strangled, and from sexual immorality. If you keep yourselves from these, you will do well.

7. What did the church in Jerusalem state was the issue affecting the Gentile believers? How were the elders choosing to deliver their response to them (see verses 24–27)?

_____

_____

_____

_____

_____

_____

_____

8. What did the church ultimately identify as the "necessary things" for the Gentile believers in Antioch to do (see verses 28–29)?

_____

_____

_____

_____

_____

_____

_____

REVIEWING THE STORY

Paul described in detail what happened when he met with Peter, James, and John—the "pillars" of the Jerusalem church. First, they *affirmed* the gospel that Paul was preaching, acknowledging it was not deficient and he did not need to add a circumcision requirement in his preaching to the Gentiles. Second, they agreed to *divide the labor*—Paul would go to the Gentiles, and they would go to the Jews. Third, they urged Paul to *remember the poor*, which may have been the very reason he and Barnabas went to Jerusalem (see Acts 11:27–30). Paul made it clear to the Judaizers that the Jerusalem apostles were in full support of his ministry. The apostles recognized the guiding hand of God in the work Paul was doing among the Gentiles.

9. Why do you think Paul spoke "privately to those who were of reputation" in the Jerusalem church (Galatians 2:2)?

_____

_____

_____

_____

_____

_____

_____

_____

10. How does Paul describe the way he resisted the false brethren who wanted to bring him into bondage (see Galatians 2:5)?

_____

_____

_____

_____

_____

_____

_____

_____

11. How did Paul describe James, Peter (whom he calls Cephas), John, and the other famous leaders of the Jerusalem church (see Galatians 2:6)?

_____

_____

_____

_____

_____

_____

12. What did James, Peter, and John perceive about Paul's ministry (see Galatians 2:9)?

_____

_____

_____

_____

_____

APPLYING THE MESSAGE

13. Are there any areas in your life where others are "spying out" the freedom you have in Christ? If so, what are some steps you can take to protect your liberty?

_____

_____

_____

_____

_____

14. What should your attitude be toward those who represent the "pillars" of Christianity in your world?

_____

_____

_____

_____

_____

_____

REFLECTING ON THE MEANING

As we read of Paul's courage for the sake of the gospel, we are reminded of the many men and women like Paul who, at a critical moment when the gospel was at stake, stood up for what was true regardless of the consequences. In some cases, their courage cost them their lives. In other cases, it cost them a loss in status, reputation, or freedom. In each case, standing up for the truth of the gospel cost them _something_. Yet they were willing to endure because they knew the gospel they proclaimed had the ability to change lives and free those in bondage.

The example of the bold Christians who have come before us should cause us to consider what our own response should be to the freedom we have received from God—and how much we treasure the relationship we have with our heavenly Father. If we truly value what we have received in Christ, it should compel us to continue to develop our relationship with our heavenly Father by spending time in His Word, in prayer, and in regularly meeting with other believers. We must continue to grow as Jesus' disciples and share the reconciliation, peace, love, and joy we have received from Him with everyone we meet.

If we are continually renewing our minds with the truths of God's Word and the reality of the gospel, then we—the body of Christ—will be able to stand by the power of the Holy Spirit and together face whatever adversity comes for the glory of His kingdom.

JOURNALING YOUR RESPONSE

In what circumstances have you boldly taken a stand in your spiritual life and refused to budge in spite of the consequences?

CONFRONTATION OVER THE GOSPEL

Galatians 2:11–21

GETTING STARTED

When is a time in your life that you experienced God's freedom?

_____

_____

_____

_____

_____

_____

_____

_____

_____

_____

_____

_____

_____

_____

_____

_____

_____

_____

SETTING THE STAGE

Up to this point, Paul has recounted for the Galatians certain experiences that led him to become the apostle to the Gentiles. These include his encounter with Jesus (see Galatians 1:15–17), his years of preparation for ministry (see 1:17–20), his visit with Barnabas to the Jerusalem church (see 2:1–2), and his complicated relationship with certain members of the Jerusalem church who could not let go of their devotion to the Law of Moses (see 2:4–5). Most of what Paul recalled took place either in Damascus, in the desert of Arabia, or in Jerusalem.

Eventually, Paul was given the "right hand of fellowship" from Peter, James, and John (see 2:9). The gesture signified the leaders of the church in Jerusalem, who perceived God's anointing on Paul, had appointed him as a minister of the gospel.

Now, in Galatians 2:11–21, the scene shifts from Jerusalem to Syria and Antioch. In the New Testament, the city of Antioch was important, as it was the church where the first Gentiles were saved, where the first mixed congregation of Jews and Gentiles was established, where Paul and Barnabas served together as co-pastors, and where the followers of Christ (formerly known as followers of "the Way") were called *Christians* for the first time.

Yet there is a stark contrast at work in this section of the letter. In the first ten verses, Paul visits Jerusalem—and Peter, James, and John give him the right hand of fellowship, encouraging him to pursue his ministry to the Gentiles. But in the next eleven verses, when Peter comes to Antioch, he refuses to eat with the "uncircumcised" Gentiles. The hypocrisy is more than Paul can take, and he calls out Peter for his actions.

EXPLORING THE TEXT

Paul Opposes Peter (Galatians 2:11–16)

---

[11] Now when Peter had come to Antioch, I withstood him to his face, because he was to be blamed; [12] for before certain men

came from James, he would eat with the Gentiles; but when they came, he withdrew and separated himself, fearing those who were of the circumcision. [13] And the rest of the Jews also played the hypocrite with him, so that even Barnabas was carried away with their hypocrisy.

[14] But when I saw that they were not straightforward about the truth of the gospel, I said to Peter before them all, "If you, being a Jew, live in the manner of Gentiles and not as the Jews, why do you compel Gentiles to live as Jews? [15] We who are Jews by nature, and not sinners of the Gentiles, [16] knowing that a man is not justified by the works of the law but by faith in Jesus Christ, even we have believed in Christ Jesus, that we might be justified by faith in Christ and not by the works of the law; for by the works of the law no flesh shall be justified."

1. What caused Peter's change of heart about eating with the Gentiles (see verses 11–12)?

2. What did Paul do when he saw the men who had been sent from James (the Jerusalem church) were not straightforward about the truth of the gospel (see verses 14–16)?

_____

_____

_____

_____

_____

_____

No Return to the Law (Galatians 2:17–21)

17 "But if, while we seek to be justified by Christ, we ourselves also are found sinners, is Christ therefore a minister of sin? Certainly not! 18 For if I build again those things which I destroyed, I make myself a transgressor. 19 For I through the law died to the law that I might live to God. 20 I have been crucified with Christ; it is no longer I who live, but Christ lives in me; and the life which I now live in the flesh I live by faith in the Son of God, who loved me and gave Himself for me. 21 I do not set aside the grace of God; for if righteousness comes through the law, then Christ died in vain."

---

3. What does Paul say happens to believers when they try to return to the law after they have destroyed its power in their lives (see verse 18)?

_____

_____

_____

_____

_____

4. What does it mean to be "crucified with Christ"? What type of transformation occurs in the life of a believer when this has taken place (see verses 19–20)?

_____

_____

_____

_____

_____

_____

_____

_____

GOING DEEPER

Many of the Gentile believers in Antioch had no reservations about eating meat the Jewish people considered ceremonially unclean—or even meat that had been offered to idols. For that reason, the church maintained two separate tables for its feasts: one for the Gentile believers and one for the Jewish believers. Peter's refusal to eat with the Gentiles served to undermine the message of the gospel that Paul was proclaiming in the church, which gave rise to Paul's sharp and severe rebuttal of Peter's actions. What is interesting is that God had already spoken to Peter about this issue in a vision before his encounter with a Gentile named Cornelius.

Peter's Vision (Acts 11:1–12)

¹ Now the apostles and brethren who were in Judea heard that the Gentiles had also received the word of God. ² And when Peter came up to Jerusalem, those of the circumcision contended with him, ³ saying, "You went in to uncircumcised men and ate with them!"

⁴ But Peter explained it to them in order from the beginning, saying: ⁵ "I was in the city of Joppa praying; and in a trance I saw a vision, an object descending like a great sheet, let down from heaven by four corners; and it came to me. ⁶ When I observed it intently and considered, I saw four-footed animals of the earth, wild beasts, creeping things, and birds of the air. ⁷ And I heard a voice saying to me, 'Rise, Peter; kill and eat.' ⁸ But I said, 'Not so, Lord! For nothing common or unclean has at any time entered my mouth.' ⁹ But the voice answered me again from heaven, 'What God has cleansed you must not call common.' ¹⁰ Now this was done three times, and all were drawn up again into heaven.

¹¹ At that very moment, three men stood before the house where I was, having been sent to me from Caesarea. ¹² Then the Spirit told me to go with them, doubting nothing. Moreover these six brethren accompanied me, and we entered the man's house.

---

5. God had given the Israelites specific instructions in the Old Testament on what foods they could eat and not eat (see Leviticus 11). How does this explain Peter's reaction to the Lord's command for him to "rise . . . kill and eat" (see Acts 11:7–8)?

6. How did God explain His command to Peter? What did this reveal to Peter about how he was to interact with the Gentiles (see verse 9)?

_____

_____

_____

_____

_____

_____

_____

_____

_____

_____

_____

_____

_____

_____

_____

_____

Peter Defends God's Grace (Acts 11:13–18)

[13] "And [Cornelius] told us how he had seen an angel standing in his house, who said to him, 'Send men to Joppa, and call for Simon whose surname is Peter, [14] who will tell you words by which you and all your household will be saved.' [15] And as I began to speak, the Holy Spirit fell upon them, as upon us at the beginning. [16] Then I remembered the word of the Lord, how He said, 'John indeed baptized with water, but you shall be baptized with the Holy Spirit.' [17] If therefore God gave them the same gift as He gave us when we believed on the Lord Jesus Christ, who was I that I could withstand God?"

[18] When they heard these things they became silent; and they glorified God, saying, "Then God has also granted to the Gentiles repentance to life."

7. How did Peter know that God had sent Cornelius (see verses 13–14)?

_____

_____

_____

_____

_____

_____

_____

_____

8. Peter states that the Holy Spirit fell on Cornelius and his men. How did this provide evidence that God had accepted them and brought them into His family (see verses 15–17)?

_____

_____

_____

_____

_____

_____

_____

_____

REVIEWING THE STORY

In this section of Galatians, we see the *cowardice of Peter* and the *courage of Paul*. The believers in Antioch had set up two tables for their congregation: one for Gentile converts and one for Jewish converts. At first, Peter had no problem sitting at the Gentile table. But when other Jewish leaders from Jerusalem arrived, he suddenly moved to the Jewish table. Other Jewish converts at Antioch, including Barnabas, followed Peter's lead. Paul confronted them about their hypocrisy and reminded them they were not justified by the law—which included following Jewish traditions—but by faith in Jesus alone.

9. According to Paul, what was at the heart of Peter's move from the Gentile table to the Jewish table (see Galatians 2:13)?

_____

_____

_____

_____

_____

_____

_____

_____

10. Why did Paul object to the Judaizers putting emphasis on the law instead of faith in Jesus Christ (see Galatians 2:16)?

_____

_____

_____

_____

_____

_____

_____

_____

11. What two things does Paul say that the Son of God does for us (see Galatians 2:20)?

12. If righteousness came through the law, what would that mean for Jesus' sacrifice on the cross (see Galatians 2:21)?

APPLYING THE MESSAGE

13. When is time that you made a decision based on peer pressure— even though you knew it was not right? How did this make you feel? How did you resolve the issue?

14. What are some examples of hypocrisy to which Christians often fall prey?

_____

_____

_____

_____

_____

_____

REFLECTING ON THE MEANING

The incident Paul relates in this section of his letter is complex, and the apostle does not provide us with all the details. We do not know the situation in the church in Antioch before and after this confrontation. Nor do we know what Peter was doing there, how long he had been there, or how the matter ultimately was resolved. What we do know is that Paul felt the need to approach his fellow believer and leader in the faith and correct him.

It is seldom easy to know when and how we are to approach other believers whom we see straying from the truth. But the account Paul relates in this section of Galatians provides us with two clear guidelines. First, the story reveals that we are to confront other believers who are in error _when the gospel is at stake._ And second, we are to confront them publicly if the offense is _public and has the potential of drawing others away from Christ._

Paul confronted Peter because his actions were not in line with "the truth of the gospel" (Galatians 2:14). For years, Peter had been a leader of the grace movement among the Jews and the Gentiles. He had been a champion of salvation by faith alone in Jesus Christ. But now, through his hypocritical actions, he had jeopardized many years of his investment.

When Paul saw this, he realized Peter's actions were sending a message to all of the Jewish Christians (and the Gentiles as well) that the most important thing was not the truth of the gospel but what other people thought about your actions. This was not a matter where Paul could simply pull Peter aside and correct him in private. Peter had acted and influenced many people in public, so Paul felt it was necessary to confront him before that very public so that they would know the truth of the gospel and what freedom in Christ really meant.

Journaling Your Response

What is the best way to respond when you see someone giving a false demonstration of what it means to be a Christian?

BEWITCHED

Galatians 3:1–14

GETTING STARTED

What is wrong with trying to earn God's favor by living a "good" life? How do you think the enemy has used this way of thinking to bewitch people?

SETTING THE STAGE

The focus of Paul's letter up to this point has been to show his readers that faith in Christ—rather than adherence to the Old Testament laws and traditions—is the only way to receive salvation. In the next section of his letter, Paul offers his arguments to support this claim. It is a crucial point in his correspondence with the believers in Galatia . . . for it is here that he must make his case for the gospel he has preached and win over the hearts and minds of his readers.

Paul begins this defense in a manner that we might not expect: by referring to the Galatians, whom he wants to persuade to his cause, as *foolish* and *bewitched*. These words of Paul are an expression of surprise, perplexity, and indignation. It was incredible to him that the Galatians were turning away from a gospel of grace to a system of legal bondage. The Galatian believers had gone from Calvary back to Mount Sinai. They had moved from sonship back to servanthood. They had moved from liberty and freedom back to bondage, from faith to works, and from Christ back to ceremonies.

In these verses, Paul offers a stark contrast between law and grace. What the great apostle wants to get across to his friends in the Galatian church is that salvation is commenced and continued in exactly the same way. The Christian begins life by faith, and it continues by faith. So many Christians believe that although they are saved by grace, they maintain their walk with God by doing good works that commend themselves to the Lord. But that is not how it works.

EXPLORING THE TEXT

Justification by Faith (Galatians 3:1–9)

¹ O foolish Galatians! Who has bewitched you that you should not obey the truth, before whose eyes Jesus Christ was clearly portrayed

among you as crucified? [2] This only I want to learn from you: Did you receive the Spirit by the works of the law, or by the hearing of faith? [3] Are you so foolish? Having begun in the Spirit, are you now being made perfect by the flesh? [4] Have you suffered so many things in vain—if indeed it was in vain?

[5] Therefore He who supplies the Spirit to you and works miracles among you, does He do it by the works of the law, or by the hearing of faith?—[6] just as Abraham "believed God, and it was accounted to him for righteousness." [7] Therefore know that only those who are of faith are sons of Abraham. [8] And the Scripture, foreseeing that God would justify the Gentiles by faith, preached the gospel to Abraham beforehand, saying, "In you all the nations shall be blessed." [9] So then those who are of faith are blessed with believing Abraham.

---

1. Why does Paul ask the Galatians to consider whether they received the Holy Spirit through the works of the law or through the message of faith he had preached to them (see verse 2)? What does he want to accomplish by reminding them of how they came to Christ?

2. Paul cites the example of Abraham—a great Old Testament hero of the faith—to show how the patriarch of the Jewish people received righteousness not by works but by faith (see verses 6–9). Given the arguments the Judaizers had made, why would this be an especially compelling illustration for the believers whom Paul was addressing?

_____

_____

_____

_____

_____

_____

_____

_____

The Law Brings a Curse (Galatians 3:10–14)

[10] For as many as are of the works of the law are under the curse; for it is written, "Cursed is everyone who does not continue in all things which are written in the book of the law, to do them." [11] But that no one is justified by the law in the sight of God is evident, for "the just shall live by faith." [12] Yet the law is not of faith, but "the man who does them shall live by them."

[13] Christ has redeemed us from the curse of the law, having become a curse for us (for it is written, "Cursed is everyone who hangs on a tree"), [14] that the blessing of Abraham might come upon the Gentiles in Christ Jesus, that we might receive the promise of the Spirit through faith.

3. In this section, Paul quotes several passages from the Old Testament that his opponents were likely using against him. What does Paul mean when he says those who seek to receive salvation by following the law are under a curse (see verses 10–11)?

4. How did Jesus "become a curse for us" (verse 13)? What is Paul saying here about the sacrifice Christ made for each of us through His death on the cross?

GOING DEEPER

The Jewish people considered Abraham to be the father of their race, and they honored him for his decision to leave his homeland and journey to the place where God had instructed. Paul recognized this fact and thus drew on the example of Abraham to counter the arguments his opponents were making about the gospel of grace. The following passage reveals the context of Genesis 15:6, the verse Paul quotes in Galatians 3:6 to prove that Abraham's *faith*—rather than just his *obedience*—led God to credit him with righteousness.

The Faith of Abraham (Genesis 15:1–6)

¹ After these things the word of the Lᴏʀᴅ came to Abram in a vision, saying, "Do not be afraid, Abram. I am your shield, your exceedingly great reward."

² But Abram said, "Lord Gᴏᴅ, what will You give me, seeing I go childless, and the heir of my house is Eliezer of Damascus?" ³ Then Abram said, "Look, You have given me no offspring; indeed one born in my house is my heir!"

⁴ And behold, the word of the Lᴏʀᴅ came to him, saying, "This one shall not be your heir, but one who will come from your own body shall be your heir." ⁵ Then He brought him outside and said, "Look now toward heaven, and count the stars if you are able to number them." And He said to him, "So shall your descendants be."

⁶ And he believed in the Lᴏʀᴅ, and He accounted it to him for righteousness.

---

5. God had promised that Abraham and Sarah would have a son in their old age . . . but many years had passed and the couple had not yet received the promised heir. What was Abraham's complaint against the Lord? How did God address this concern (see verses 1–4)?

_____

_____

_____

_____

_____

_____

6. Throughout Genesis, the author points out that it was Abraham's *faith* that enabled him to be used by God. How does this fact support Paul's argument that faith in Jesus is the decisive factor for our salvation?

_____

_____

_____

_____

_____

_____

Paul was not the only New Testament author to use the story of Abraham as an example of a person who received great blessings from the Lord because of his *faith*. In the book of Hebrews, the writer also cites the example of Abraham to show the power of faith and how God rewards those who choose to believe in Him . . . in spite of the consequences.

A Life of Faith (Hebrews 11:8–16)

8 By faith Abraham obeyed when he was called to go out to the place which he would receive as an inheritance. And he went out, not knowing where he was going. 9 By faith he dwelt in the land of promise as in a foreign country, dwelling in tents with Isaac and Jacob, the heirs with him of the same promise; 10 for he waited for the city which has foundations, whose builder and maker is God.

11 By faith Sarah herself also received strength to conceive seed, and she bore a child when she was past the age, because she judged Him faithful who had promised. 12 Therefore from one man, and him as good as dead, were born as many as the stars of the sky in multitude—innumerable as the sand which is by the seashore.

13 These all died in faith, not having received the promises, but having seen them afar off were assured of them, embraced them and confessed that they were strangers and pilgrims on the earth. 14 For

those who say such things declare plainly that they seek a homeland. [15] And truly if they had called to mind that country from which they had come out, they would have had opportunity to return. [16] But now they desire a better, that is, a heavenly country. Therefore God is not ashamed to be called their God, for He has prepared a city for them.

---

7. What are some of the things Abraham and Sarah did by faith (see verses 8–11)?

_____

_____

_____

_____

_____

8. Abraham's decision to follow God meant a nomadic lifestyle in which he was often considered a stranger and pilgrim on this earth— yet God rewarded him with an eternal home. How does this illustration relate to the life of a believer in Christ?

_____

_____

_____

_____

_____

REVIEWING THE STORY

Paul called the Galatians *foolish* and *bewitched* for choosing to embrace the law instead of the promise of God's grace. He stated that those who fail to live up to the standard of the law put themselves under a curse and a penalty for their failure. Only Jesus Christ could live up to this standard, so only

He could provide the means to escape the curse. Therefore, those who attempt to live up to the law, rather than put their faith in Jesus' sacrifice for their sins, are truly foolish in their decision to condemn themselves. Paul also reminded the believers they had received the Holy Spirit through *faith*, not the law, and drew on the example of Abraham to show how God considered him righteous because of his *faith*.

9. Who does Paul say are the "sons of Abraham" (see Galatians 3:7)?

_____

_____

_____

_____

_____

10. What did the Scriptures foresee regarding Abraham (see Galatians 3:8)?

_____

_____

_____

_____

_____

_____

11. If no one is justified by the law . . . how shall the just live (see Galatians 3:11)?

_____

_____

_____

_____

12. How do we receive the promise of the Spirit (see Galatians 3:14)?

APPLYING THE MESSAGE

13. Why do Christians sometimes feel as though they have to earn God's favor?

14. How has God strengthened your faith since the time you accepted Christ as your Savior?

Reflecting on the Meaning

The Bible is clear that all of us have missed the mark when it comes to living up to the standards of God's law. As Paul wrote:

> There is none righteous, no, not one . . . for all have sinned and
> fall short of the glory of God (Romans 3:10, 23).

All have sinned—there are no exceptions—and the consequences of that "sin is death" (6:23). Furthermore, the Bible is clear there is *nothing* we can do on our own to save ourselves from that penalty of sin.

This is the hard reality of our situation as fallen human beings. But the amazing reality of God's grace is that He offers us a pardon for our sin. For though none of us could ever live up to God's standard, there is One who lived on this earth who could . . . and did. Jesus was human just like us, and faced the same challenges as we do to sin, and yet He lived a perfect life. It is because of this simple fact that He was able to be the perfect sacrifice to pay for our sins. As the author of Hebrews put it, "For by one offering He has perfected forever those who are being sanctified" (Hebrews 10:14).

Paul called the believers in Galatia *bewitched* because they had been duped into believing they could somehow live up to God's perfect standard in the law . . . that if they just tried harder, they could be acceptable to God. But the reality is that God's grace had already been extended to them, they had accepted Jesus' sacrifice for their sins, and they were living as new creations in Christ. God had accepted them and adopted them into His family.

The enemy likes to bewitch us into thinking salvation comes through our efforts. But when we understand the depth of what Jesus did for us on the cross, it allows us to say to God, "Lord, I know You have accepted me, and there is nothing I can do to be more accepted. I want to live in light of that truth. When people look at me, I want them to see You have accepted me—and know that they can also choose to be a part of Your family."

JOURNALING YOUR RESPONSE

What is the most effective motivation in your life when it comes to growing in your relationship with God?

THE LAW AND
THE PROMISE

Galatians 3:15–29

GETTING STARTED

What do you feel is the most divisive issue in the church today?

_____

_____

_____

_____

_____

_____

_____

_____

_____

_____

_____

_____

_____

SETTING THE STAGE

In Paul's day, just like our own, people in the church faced issues that
threatened to divide their congregations. In fact, one of the reasons we

have the letters in the New Testament is because the churches at the time had so many problems—and leaders like Paul were compelled to address those concerns and stamp out any false teachings before they led to greater error.

As we have seen, one of the main issues confronting the Galatians was the question of whether the Gentiles needed to adopt Jewish practices in order to be Christians. Up to this point in his letter, Paul has pointed out the error in believing that following the law—or, rather, attempting to do so—has any power to save a person. While Paul did not try to dissuade Jewish believers from engaging in such traditions or practices, he did not feel it was right to impose such obligations on the Gentile believers. For Paul, only *faith in Jesus* can save a person.

In this next section of his letter, Paul addresses the questions he knows his arguments will raise: *If the law is not required for salvation . . . then what good is it? Why would God give the law to humankind if it could not save anyone? What was the purpose of the law anyway?*

To answer these questions, Paul offers four statements to help his readers understand the relationship between the *promise* made to Abraham and the *law* given to Moses. First, *the law is incidental to the promise*: the promise was given some 430 years before the law. Second, *the law is inferior to the promise*: the law is temporary, while the promise is permanent. Third, *the law is important to the promise*: the law demonstrates our sinfulness and drives us to Christ. Finally, *the law is inclusive, and so is the promise*: we are all sinners under the law—and we can all be participants in the promise.

EXPLORING THE TEXT

The Changeless Promise (Galatians 3:15–18)

---

[15] Brethren, I speak in the manner of men: Though it is only a man's covenant, yet if it is confirmed, no one annuls or adds to it. [16] Now to Abraham and his Seed were the promises made. He does not

say, "And to seeds," as of many, but as of one, "And to your Seed," who is Christ. ¹⁷ And this I say, that the law, which was four hundred and thirty years later, cannot annul the covenant that was confirmed before by God in Christ, that it should make the promise of no effect. ¹⁸ For if the inheritance is of the law, it is no longer of promise; but God gave it to Abraham by promise.

---

1. Paul begins by stating that a contract between people—once executed—is binding and cannot be changed. How does this analogy relate to the point he is making about the covenant or "contract" God had with Abraham and his Seed (see verses 15–16)?

_____

_____

_____

_____

_____

2. Paul notes the covenant God made with Abraham—in which God said "all the families of the earth shall be blessed" through him (Genesis 12:3)—took place some 430 years before the law was given (see Galatians 3:17). What point is Paul making when he states this covenant cannot be annulled by the law? How does this relate to the Gentile believers?

_____

_____

_____

_____

_____

Purpose of the Law (Galatians 3:19–29)

[19] What purpose then does the law serve? It was added because of transgressions, till the Seed should come to whom the promise was made; and it was appointed through angels by the hand of a mediator. [20] Now a mediator does not mediate for one only, but God is one.

[21] Is the law then against the promises of God? Certainly not! For if there had been a law given which could have given life, truly righteousness would have been by the law. [22] But the Scripture has confined all under sin, that the promise by faith in Jesus Christ might be given to those who believe. [23] But before faith came, we were kept under guard by the law, kept for the faith which would afterward be revealed. [24] Therefore the law was our tutor to bring us to Christ, that we might be justified by faith. [25] But after faith has come, we are no longer under a tutor.

[26] For you are all sons of God through faith in Christ Jesus. [27] For as many of you as were baptized into Christ have put on Christ. [28] There is neither Jew nor Greek, there is neither slave nor free, there is neither male nor female; for you are all one in Christ Jesus. [29] And if you are Christ's, then you are Abraham's seed, and heirs according to the promise.

3. According to the apostle Paul, what was the purpose of the law (see verses 21–24)?

_____

_____

_____

_____

_____

_____

_____

4. The law served to separate the Israelites from their pagan neighbors and show their commitment to following God and His ways. What did Paul say had changed in this system? What does it mean that "all are one in Christ Jesus" (see verses 26–29)?

_____

_____

_____

_____

_____

_____

_____

_____

_____

_____

_____

GOING DEEPER

Paul's argument in this portion of his letter is that God made a covenant long before the law was given. This greater covenant pointed to the arrival of Abraham's "Seed"—whom Paul identified as Christ, the only one who could fulfill all the terms of the law. The following passage outlines this promise that God made to Abraham—which Paul notes extends to all people, including the Gentiles.

The Sign of the Covenant (Genesis 17:1–8)

¹ When Abram was ninety-nine years old, the LORD appeared to Abram and said to him, "I am Almighty God; walk before Me and be blameless. ² And I will make My covenant between Me and you, and will multiply you exceedingly." ³ Then Abram fell on his face, and God talked with him, saying: ⁴ "As for Me, behold, My covenant is

with you, and you shall be a father of many nations. ⁵ No longer shall your name be called Abram, but your name shall be Abraham; for I have made you a father of many nations. ⁶ I will make you exceedingly fruitful; and I will make nations of you, and kings shall come from you. ⁷ And I will establish My covenant between Me and you and your descendants after you in their generations, for an everlasting covenant, to be God to you and your descendants after you. ⁸ Also I give to you and your descendants after you the land in which you are a stranger, all the land of Canaan, as an everlasting possession; and I will be their God."

---

5. What promise did God make to Abraham? What was significant in God changing his name from "Abram," which means *exalted father*, to "Abraham," which means *father of a multitude* (see verses 2–5)?

6. What is significant about the fact this promise was made to Abraham long before the arrival of the law?

_____

_____

_____

_____

_____

_____

_____

_____

_____

Paul mentions that the law required a mediator: "The law . . . was appointed through angels by the hand of a mediator" (Galatians 3:19). While the law was mediated by angels, the grace is mediated by Jesus. In the book of Hebrews, the author reveals that Jesus serves as the mediator, or high priest, or the New Covenant.

Our Great High Priest (Hebrews 10:19–25)

[19] Therefore, brethren, having boldness to enter the Holiest by the blood of Jesus, [20] by a new and living way which He consecrated for us, through the veil, that is, His flesh, [21] and having a High Priest over the house of God, [22] let us draw near with a true heart in full assurance of faith, having our hearts sprinkled from an evil conscience and our bodies washed with pure water. [23] Let us hold fast the confession of our hope without wavering, for He who promised is faithful. [24] And let us consider one another in order to stir up love and good works, [25] not forsaking the assembling of ourselves together, as is the manner of some, but exhorting one another, and so much the more as you see the Day approaching.

7. The "Holiest" or "Holy of Holies" refers to the inner sanctuary within the Temple where God's presence appeared. The area was separated from the main sanctuary by two curtains, and only the high priest could enter once a year on the Day of Atonement. Why can believers in Christ now enter into the Holy of Holies (see verses 19–21)?

_____

_____

_____

_____

_____

_____

_____

_____

8. How does Jesus serve as a high priest for those who put their faith in Him? How does His sacrifice on the cross allow us to boldly enter the presence of God (see verses 22–23)?

_____

_____

_____

_____

_____

_____

_____

_____

REVIEWING THE STORY

Paul helped the Galatian believers understand that God had made a promise to Abraham and his Seed. The law, which God gave to Moses hundreds of years later, could not override that promise. However, Paul notes the law does serve important purposes. It helps us recognize our weakness and sinfulness. It shows us that we cannot achieve salvation through our works. Most importantly, the law served as a tutor to bring us to Christ. The promise is available to all who are in the body of Christ—regardless of gender, race, or any other difference.

9. Paul states, "Now to Abraham and his Seed were the promises made" (Galatians 3:16). Who is the Seed? What role does He play in the covenant God made?

_____

_____

_____

_____

_____

_____

_____

10. How many years passed between God's giving of the promise to Abraham and His giving of the law to Moses? Why is this significant (see Galatians 3:17)?

_____

_____

_____

_____

_____

_____

_____

11. What role did the law serve? What changed after Christ came (see Galatians 3:23)?

_____

_____

_____

_____

_____

_____

12. What point is Paul making by his statement that within the body of Christ, there are no divisions or classes of people—for all are one (see Galatians 3:25)?

_____

_____

_____

_____

_____

_____

_____

APPLYING THE MESSAGE

13. How would you explain to someone the difference between the law and the promise?

_____

_____

_____

_____

_____

_____

14. Why is it important to consider everyone equal within the body of Christ?

_____

_____

_____

_____

_____

_____

_____

REFLECTING ON THE MEANING

As Paul notes, *everything* changes when we are redeemed from the prison of sin through the pardon we receive in Jesus Christ. All spiritual differences are abolished—"There is neither Jew nor Greek, there is neither slave nor free, there is neither male nor female" (Galatians 3:28). In other word, all believers have equal standing before God as His children. Not one of us is any better than the rest. We are all together as one in His family.

Notice the way Paul goes on to describe this new family—in terms of its height, depth, width, and length. In *height*, this family reaches all the way up to God in heaven (see verse 26). In *depth*, it reaches all the way down to our baptism into Christ and our identification with Him (see verse 27). In *width*, it is all together—we are all one in Christ (see verse 28). In *length*, it starts right where we are today and stretches all the way back to Abraham.

The Bible says if we are children of faith—if we have accepted the sacrifice of Christ for our sins—we are the children of Abraham. The same promise God gave to Abraham is extended to *all* who share in the faith. So, now that we are in the church, we are related to God in heaven. We are related to Christ in baptism. We are related to one another in the church. And we are related to Abraham in the promise that God made with him.

JOURNALING YOUR RESPONSE

What is most meaningful to you about being part of the family of God?

TIME TO GROW UP

Galatians 4:1–20

GETTING STARTED

What tradition or custom in your family would you like to end—or at least change?

SETTING THE STAGE

For the apostle Paul, the Law of Moses served as a form of an instructor or tutor. You can think of it in terms of attending classes when you were in high school. You received instruction from your teacher. You hopefully learned the lessons. You then took a test to see if the information had stuck—and whether you had passed the standards set by the teacher. Sometimes, you scored well on the test. Other times, you realized you still had much to learn . . . and the test had revealed just how short you had fallen of the standard.

In the same way, the Law of Moses served as an instructor to the people of God before the coming of Christ. It revealed God's standards to those who wished to follow Him. It instructed them on just how sinful they were before Him and how they needed His mercy and grace. The law was a *guardian* that protected the Israelites by showing what God expected of them—but it was only intended to lead them until the time of Jesus' arrival.

In this next section, Paul continues to tackle this aspect of the Old Testament law and shows how it fit in with God's plan of redemption through Christ. It is clear that Paul saw a contrast between the age of immaturity, characterized by the supervision of the law, and the age of maturity, which people could now enter through faith in Christ and the guidance of the Holy Spirit that would dwell within them. Believers were free from tutelage of the law and now under the guidance of Christ.

As Paul would write to another congregation:

> You also have become dead to the law through the body of Christ, that you might be married to another—to Him who was raised from the dead (Romans 7:4).

The law had its place . . . but the law now was dead, and Christ had come. In its place was something far better: spiritual *adoption* into God's own family.

EXPLORING THE TEXT

Sons and Heirs Through Christ (Galatians 4:1–7)

¹ Now I say that the heir, as long as he is a child, does not differ at all from a slave, though he is master of all, ² but is under guardians and stewards until the time appointed by the father. ³ Even so we, when we were children, were in bondage under the elements of the world. ⁴ But when the fullness of the time had come, God sent forth His Son, born of a woman, born under the law, ⁵ to redeem those who were under the law, that we might receive the adoption as sons.

⁶ And because you are sons, God has sent forth the Spirit of His Son into your hearts, crying out, "Abba, Father!" ⁷ Therefore you are no longer a slave but a son, and if a son, then an heir of God through Christ.

1. Paul uses the legal terminology of his day to illustrate how believers have moved from the age of the law to the age of grace in Christ. In what ways is an heir to a great inheritance just like a servant in the household before he comes of age (see verses 1–3)?

2. What allowed us to come of age and receive our inheritance? How has Christ redeemed those who were under the law (see verses 4–5)?

_____

_____

_____

_____

_____

Fears for the Church (Galatians 4:8–20)

⁸ But then, indeed, when you did not know God, you served those which by nature are not gods. ⁹ But now after you have known God, or rather are known by God, how is it that you turn again to the weak and beggarly elements, to which you desire again to be in bondage? ¹⁰ You observe days and months and seasons and years. ¹¹ I am afraid for you, lest I have labored for you in vain.

¹² Brethren, I urge you to become like me, for I became like you. You have not injured me at all. ¹³ You know that because of physical infirmity I preached the gospel to you at the first. ¹⁴ And my trial which was in my flesh you did not despise or reject, but you received me as an angel of God, even as Christ Jesus. ¹⁵ What then was the blessing you enjoyed? For I bear you witness that, if possible, you would have plucked out your own eyes and given them to me. ¹⁶ Have I therefore become your enemy because I tell you the truth?

¹⁷ They zealously court you, but for no good; yes, they want to exclude you, that you may be zealous for them. ¹⁸ But it is good to be zealous in a good thing always, and not only when I am present with you. ¹⁹ My little children, for whom I labor in birth again until Christ is formed in you, ²⁰ I would like to be present with you now and to change my tone; for I have doubts about you.

3. Paul reminds the Galatians that before they came to Christ, they engaged in the ritualistic practices of their pagan culture, worshiping idols and spirits. What point is he making when he then asks, "How is it that you turn again to the weak and beggarly elements, to which you desire again to be in bondage" (verse 9)?

_____

_____

_____

_____

_____

_____

_____

_____

4. How does Paul describe his motives when he was among the Galatians? How does he describe the motives of the Judaizers (see verses 13–17)?

_____

_____

_____

_____

_____

_____

_____

_____

_____

_____

GOING DEEPER

The issue of whether Gentile believers needed to adopt Jewish practices was prevalent in many first-century Christian churches. In Paul's letter to the churches in Rome, we again see him addressing this issue and calling out the fact that Jesus—as the only perfect human being to ever live—fulfilled the requirements of the law so we could receive freedom from the penalty of sin. As Paul notes, the question is what we will do now that we have received this freedom. Will we walk in step with the Holy Spirit, or will we walk according to our former ways and the flesh?

Freedom from Sin (Romans 8:1–11)

[1] There is therefore now no condemnation to those who are in Christ Jesus, who do not walk according to the flesh, but according to the Spirit. [2] For the law of the Spirit of life in Christ Jesus has made me free from the law of sin and death. [3] For what the law could not do in that it was weak through the flesh, God did by sending His own Son in the likeness of sinful flesh, on account of sin: He condemned sin in the flesh, [4] that the righteous requirement of the law might be fulfilled in us who do not walk according to the flesh but according to the Spirit. [5] For those who live according to the flesh set their minds on the things of the flesh, but those who live according to the Spirit, the things of the Spirit. [6] For to be carnally minded is death, but to be spiritually minded is life and peace. [7] Because the carnal mind is enmity against God; for it is not subject to the law of God, nor indeed can be. [8] So then, those who are in the flesh cannot please God.

[9] But you are not in the flesh but in the Spirit, if indeed the Spirit of God dwells in you. Now if anyone does not have the Spirit of Christ, he is not His. [10] And if Christ is in you, the body is dead because of sin, but the Spirit is life because of righteousness. [11] But if the Spirit of Him who raised Jesus from the dead dwells in you,

He who raised Christ from the dead will also give life to your mortal bodies through His Spirit who dwells in you.

---

5. Paul notes the law makes demands and condemns when those demands are not met, but it cannot overcome sin. So how do we gain freedom from sin (see verses 2–4)?

_____

_____

_____

_____

_____

_____

_____

6. How does Paul say a believer is empowered to not walk in the flesh (see verses 9–11)?

_____

_____

_____

_____

_____

_____

Sonship Through the Spirit (Romans 8:12–17)

12 Therefore, brethren, we are debtors—not to the flesh, to live according to the flesh. 13 For if you live according to the flesh you will die; but if by the Spirit you put to death the deeds of the body, you will live. 14 For as many as are led by the Spirit of God, these are sons of God. 15 For you did not receive the spirit of bondage again

to fear, but you received the Spirit of adoption by whom we cry out, "Abba, Father." [16] The Spirit Himself bears witness with our spirit that we are children of God, [17] and if children, then heirs—heirs of God and joint heirs with Christ, if indeed we suffer with Him, that we may also be glorified together.

7. What happens when we choose to live according to the flesh? What happens when we choose to be led by the Spirit (see verses 12–14)?

8. What similarities do you find between Paul's words in Romans 8:15–17 and Galatians 4:6–7? What is the key point that Paul is making?

REVIEWING THE STORY

Paul used the analogy of an heir under the watchful eye of a guardian to describe the purpose of the law. As long as the heir is a child, he does not differ from a servant in the household. But when he comes of age, he leaves the guardian and steps into his inheritance. Paul was amazed that the Galatians, who had experienced the freedom of Christ, were choosing to return to the bondage of the law. He reminded them that Jesus had made it possible for them to be adopted as His children. On a personal level, Paul then asked what had happened to his relationship with them. They had welcomed him so warmly, in spite of his physical infirmities, but now it seemed he had become their enemy because he spoke the truth.

9. What was our condition when we were spiritual "children" (see Galatians 4:3)?

_____

_____

_____

_____

_____

_____

_____

10. What happens when God's Spirit enters into our hearts (see Galatians 4:6–7)?

_____

_____

_____

_____

_____

_____

_____

11. What was the difference between what the Galatians were doing before they knew God and what they were doing after they knew Him (see Galatians 4:8–9)?

12. What extreme image does Paul use to describe the Galatians' generous spirit toward him when he first arrived (see Galatians 4:15)?

APPLYING THE MESSAGE

13. What does it mean in your daily life that you are a beloved child and heir of God?

14. What is the best strategy for dealing with someone who treats you as an enemy when you tell him or her the truth?

_____

_____

_____

_____

_____

_____

_____

REFLECTING ON THE MEANING

It is important for us as believers in Christ to acknowledge the significance of the law and why it was given in the Old Testament. Yet it is also crucial for us to understand the powerlessness of the law to save us from the bondage of sin. The law cannot make us righteous, because the law merely shows us what we are incapable of doing. The law points out and reveals our sinfulness. The law serves as a guardian—instructing us as to what God expects and correcting us when we stray from the path.

Fortunately, God didn't leave us with the law as our guide to navigate life. He gave us the Holy Spirit to dwell within our hearts and help us honor and serve Him as His redeemed children. The Holy Spirit convicts us of our sin and guides us in living according to God's purposes. He is the Comforter . . . but He is also the "Discomforter." When we choose to follow the way of the flesh and stray from God's path, the Holy Spirit lets us know.

The Holy Spirit brings not only conviction but also power into our lives. We couldn't live the Christian life by our own energy any more than we could receive salvation by our own energy. But we have a new power that we didn't have before we trusted in Jesus as our Savior. We now have an internal source of power—the very Spirit of the living God.

JOURNALING YOUR RESPONSE

When has the Holy Spirit made you uncomfortable? How have you seen
His power in your life?

LESSON *eight*

A TALE OF TWO SONS

Galatians 4:21–31

GETTING STARTED

What does Christian freedom mean to you?

_____

_____

_____

_____

_____

_____

_____

_____

_____

_____

_____

_____

_____

_____

_____

_____

_____

_____

_____

_____

_____

SETTING THE STAGE

Paul has been arguing that salvation and freedom from sin come through *faith in Christ alone*, not by following the law. In this passage, he returns to the Old Testament to point out the difference between the gospel of grace he had preached to the Galatian believers and the gospel of the law the Judaizers were promoting. As before, the story involves Abraham, the father of the Jewish race. But this time it focuses on Abraham and his two sons.

At the center of Paul's message is the number *two*. Abraham has *two* sons: Ishmael and Isaac. These sons are born of *two* different women: a slave woman named Hagar and a free woman named Sarah. The accounts of these two women and their sons represent *two* different covenants: the law and the promise. Furthermore, these covenants point to *two* different outcomes: one that gives birth to bondage (symbolically represented by the earthly Jerusalem), and one that gives birth to freedom (symbolically represented by the heavenly Jerusalem). Two different stories . . . leading to two different ends.

Paul sums up his point by asking, "Tell me, you who desire to be under the law, do you not hear the law?" (Galatians 4:21). In other words, Paul is saying, "So, you want to be under the law, but do you even *know* what the law says? Do you know to what outcome that will lead?" Paul's message is clear—it is better to be a child of the promise than a child of the law!

EXPLORING THE TEXT

Two Covenants (Galatians 4:21–27)

---

21 Tell me, you who desire to be under the law, do you not hear the law? 22 For it is written that Abraham had two sons: the one by a bondwoman, the other by a freewoman. 23 But he who was of the bondwoman was born according to the flesh, and he of the freewoman through promise, 24 which things are symbolic. For these are the two covenants: the one from Mount Sinai which gives birth to

bondage, which is Hagar—[25] for this Hagar is Mount Sinai in Arabia, and corresponds to Jerusalem which now is, and is in bondage with her children—[26] but the Jerusalem above is free, which is the mother of us all. [27] For it is written:

> "Rejoice, O barren,
> You who do not bear!
> Break forth and shout,
> You who are not in labor!
> For the desolate has many more children
> Than she who has a husband."

1. How does Paul describe the difference between Abraham's two sons (see verses 22–23)?

_____

_____

_____

_____

_____

_____

2. What is the difference between the two covenants—the one from Mount Sinai and the one from the heavenly Jerusalem (see verses 24–26)?

_____

_____

_____

_____

_____

_____

_____

_____

Children of Promise (Galatians 4:28–31)

28 Now we, brethren, as Isaac was, are children of promise. 29 But, as he who was born according to the flesh then persecuted him who was born according to the Spirit, even so it is now. 30 Nevertheless what does the Scripture say? "Cast out the bondwoman and her son, for the son of the bondwoman shall not be heir with the son of the freewoman." 31 So then, brethren, we are not children of the bondwoman but of the free.

3. How were the apostle Paul and the Galatian believers similar to Isaac (see verse 28)?

_____

_____

_____

_____

_____

_____

4. How was the situation between Ishmael and Isaac similar to the situation between the Judaizers and the Galatian believers (see verse 29)?

_____

_____

_____

_____

_____

GOING DEEPER

The Jewish people held Abraham in high esteem because of his dedicated faith in God—a faith that led him to leave his homeland, enter into a covenant with God, and believe for more than twenty-five years that the Lord would fulfill His promise of giving him a son. However, Abraham was a human being like us who made mistakes. Perhaps his greatest mistake was the decision to "help out" God's plan by having a son with his servant Hagar. The following passage gives the background for Abraham's decision and provides context for Paul's claim to the Galatians of the two "covenants"—that of the promise and of the law.

Abraham and Sarah's Plan (Genesis 16:1–6)

¹ Now Sarai, Abram's wife, had borne him no children. And she had an Egyptian maidservant whose name was Hagar. ² So Sarai said to Abram, "See now, the LORD has restrained me from bearing children. Please, go in to my maid; perhaps I shall obtain children by her." And Abram heeded the voice of Sarai. ³ Then Sarai, Abram's wife, took Hagar her maid, the Egyptian, and gave her to her husband Abram to be his wife, after Abram had dwelt ten years in the land of Canaan. ⁴ So he went in to Hagar, and she conceived. And when she saw that she had conceived, her mistress became despised in her eyes.

⁵ Then Sarai said to Abram, "My wrong be upon you! I gave my maid into your embrace; and when she saw that she had conceived, I became despised in her eyes. The LORD judge between you and me."

⁶ So Abram said to Sarai, "Indeed your maid is in your hand; do to her as you please." And when Sarai dealt harshly with her, she fled from her presence.

5. What was the strategy that Sarah (called Sarai in this passage) devised for fulfilling God's promise of an heir (see verses 1–4)? What was her reason for making this decision?

_____

_____

_____

_____

_____

_____

_____

6. What happened after Hagar had given birth to Abraham's son (see verses 4–6)?

_____

_____

_____

_____

_____

_____

_____

_____

The Prophecy Concerning Ishmael (Genesis 16:7–16)

7 Now the Angel of the Lord found her by a spring of water in the wilderness, by the spring on the way to Shur. 8 And He said, "Hagar, Sarai's maid, where have you come from, and where are you going?"

She said, "I am fleeing from the presence of my mistress Sarai."

9 The Angel of the Lord said to her, "Return to your mistress, and submit yourself under her hand." 10 Then the Angel of the Lord

said to her, "I will multiply your descendants exceedingly, so that they shall not be counted for multitude." ¹¹ And the Angel of the LORD said to her:

> "Behold, you are with child,
> And you shall bear a son.
> You shall call his name Ishmael,
> Because the LORD has heard your affliction.
> ¹² He shall be a wild man;
> His hand shall be against every man,
> And every man's hand against him.
> And he shall dwell in the presence of all his brethren."

¹³ Then she called the name of the LORD who spoke to her, You-Are-the-God-Who-Sees; for she said, "Have I also here seen Him who sees me?" ¹⁴ Therefore the well was called Beer Lahai Roi; observe, it is between Kadesh and Bered.

¹⁵ So Hagar bore Abram a son; and Abram named his son, whom Hagar bore, Ishmael. ¹⁶ Abram was eighty-six years old when Hagar bore Ishmael to Abram.

---

7. What instruction did the Lord give to Hagar in the wilderness? Why might God have told her to take this course of action (see verses 7–9)?

_____

_____

_____

_____

_____

_____

_____

_____

8. What prophecy did the Lord give to Hagar concerning the son she would bear to Abraham (see verses 11–12)?

_____

_____

_____

_____

_____

_____

REVIEWING THE STORY

Ishmael was born to Hagar, a bondwoman, when Abraham and Sarah decided to rush God's plan for a promised son. Later, Isaac was born to Sarah, a freewoman, when Abraham and Sarah decided to wait for God's plan to unfold. Paul uses this story to portray two different types of covenants—one with Ishmael, representing the covenant of the law (which leads to bondage), and one with Isaac, representing the covenant of promise (which leads to freedom). Paul's point was that believers in Christ are children of the freewoman, while those who seek to follow the law are children of the bondwoman.

9. According to Paul, what was the result of the covenant of Mount Sinai (see Galatians 4:24)?

_____

_____

_____

_____

_____

_____

10. What was the result of the covenant of the heavenly Jerusalem above (see Galatians 4:26)?

_____

_____

_____

_____

_____

_____

11. How did Paul describe Ishmael, who was born to Hagar (see Galatians 4:29)?

_____

_____

_____

_____

_____

_____

12. What did Paul say the Galatian believers should do with the Judaizers (see Galatians 4:30)?

_____

_____

_____

_____

_____

_____

APPLYING THE MESSAGE

13. Where in your life are you still living in bondage?

_____

_____

_____

_____

_____

_____

_____

_____

14. What does it mean to you to be a child of the promise?

_____

_____

_____

_____

_____

_____

_____

_____

_____

REFLECTING ON THE MEANING

Paul provides several principles which help us understand how the story of Ishmael and Isaac applies to our Christian experience. First, *we are children of promise* (see Galatians 4:28). Isaac's birth was based not on *performance* but on *promise*. God deliberately waited twenty-five years to fulfill His promise to Abraham and Sarah. The Lord wanted there to be no doubt about the nature of Isaac's miraculous birth.

Paul was essentially stating to his readers, "We are born again solely by faith. Just as the works of the law had nothing to do with Isaac's birth, so the works of the law have nothing to do with our spiritual birth." We are never to forget we are children of God through the miraculous new birth that God has provided for us. We did not do anything to obtain this status before God. We were just as unable to produce this new life as Abraham and Sarah were unable to produce an heir in their old age. God does a miracle in our lives.

Second, as children of the promise, *we become candidates for persecution.* Paul writes that "he who was born according to the flesh then persecuted him who was born according to the Spirit" (verse 29). Paul is likely referring to the time Sarah saw Hagar mocking Isaac (see Genesis 21:9). As believers who are a part of God's family—as children of the promise—we should expect to be persecuted. As Paul later wrote, "All who desire to live godly in Christ Jesus will suffer persecution" (2 Timothy 3:12).

Finally, *we are not to compromise with the flesh.* In verse 30, Paul writes, "Cast out the bondwoman and her son, for the son of the bondwoman shall not be heir with the son of the freewoman.'" When Sarah saw Ishmael mocking Isaac, she demanded the immediate expulsion of Hagar and her son. Under God's direct command, Abraham reluctantly did what Sarah desired. Ishmael was banished once and for all by Divine decree from the place of promise.

Paul is telling the Galatians that bringing the works of the law back into place after Christ is akin to bringing Hagar and Ishmael back into the fold. It is impossible and is an affront to God. You cannot mix law and grace any more than you can reconcile Hagar and Sarah, Ishmael and Isaac. The flesh cannot keep God's law. All the legalists were offering the Galatians was an invitation to saddle themselves with not only the Law of Moses but also the endless rules of the rabbis. All these things were to be kept in the energy of the flesh. This is antithetical to the gospel of Jesus Christ.

Journaling Your Response

What ideas about salvation and good works do you need to cast out today so you can better experience the freedom you have been given in Christ?

LESSON *nine*

THE LAW OF LIBERTY
Galatians 5:1–15

GETTING STARTED

What are some spiritual disciplines you follow that have helped you grow in your faith?

_____

_____

_____

_____

_____

_____

_____

_____

_____

_____

_____

_____

_____

_____

_____

_____

_____

SETTING THE STAGE

In this section of Paul's appeal to the Galatian believers, he reminds them of a simple yet profound truth: through faith in Christ, they have been *set free* from the bondage of sin and the tyranny of legalism. Their faith in Christ has granted them liberty from the frustration of trying to perfectly keep the law . . . all the while knowing they never could. Jesus has freed them from the pressure of trying to earn God's favor. Through His sacrifice, they can know they are completely accepted by God.

In making this argument, Paul was repeating a message that Jesus had stated to His followers during His ministry on earth. After giving thanks to God for them, He proclaimed, "Come to Me, all you who labor and are heavy laden, and I will give you rest. Take My yoke upon you and learn from Me, for I am gentle and lowly in heart, and you will find rest for your souls. For My yoke is easy and My burden is light" (Matthew 11:28–30).

The Judaizers were attempting to compel the Galatians to become "entangled again with a yoke of bondage" (Galatians 5:1). They were trying to shackle the believers again with human-made rules and regulations. Paul calls the Galatians to not only cast out this false doctrine but also to stand fast against it. He wants them to put up a solid front and not yield an inch to accepting this error as the truth.

Paul knew standing fast is never easy. But freedom requires us to move from the rules and regulations of bondage to the firm trust and love found in a relationship with Christ. As we do, we are able to receive the love of Jesus and, in turn, fulfill what He said was the greatest commandment: "Love your neighbor as yourself" (verse 14).

EXPLORING THE TEXT

Liberty in Christ (Galatians 5:1–6)

¹ Stand fast therefore in the liberty by which Christ has made us free, and do not be entangled again with a yoke of bondage.

² Indeed I, Paul, say to you that if you become circumcised, Christ will profit you nothing. ³ And I testify again to every man who becomes circumcised that he is a debtor to keep the whole law. ⁴ You have become estranged from Christ, you who attempt to be justified by law; you have fallen from grace. ⁵ For we through the Spirit eagerly wait for the hope of righteousness by faith. ⁶ For in Christ Jesus neither circumcision nor uncircumcision avails anything, but faith working through love.

---

1. What two things did Paul warn would happen if the Galatians submitted to circumcision and chose to again be under the yoke of the law (see verses 2–3)?

_____

_____

_____

_____

_____

_____

2. After Paul details the consequences of submitting to the law, how does he describe the Spirit-filled life (see verses 5–6)?

_____

_____

_____

_____

_____

_____

_____

Love Fulfills the Law (Galatians 5:7–15)

⁷ You ran well. Who hindered you from obeying the truth? ⁸ This persuasion does not come from Him who calls you. ⁹ A little leaven leavens the whole lump. ¹⁰ I have confidence in you, in the Lord, that you will have no other mind; but he who troubles you shall bear his judgment, whoever he is.

¹¹ And I, brethren, if I still preach circumcision, why do I still suffer persecution? Then the offense of the cross has ceased. ¹² I could wish that those who trouble you would even cut themselves off!

¹³ For you, brethren, have been called to liberty; only do not use liberty as an opportunity for the flesh, but through love serve one another. ¹⁴ For all the law is fulfilled in one word, even in this: "You shall love your neighbor as yourself." ¹⁵ But if you bite and devour one another, beware lest you be consumed by one another.

3. What does Paul mean when he states that the believers "ran well" (verse 7)? What tone do you sense here in his words to his readers?

4. How were the Galatians to use the freedom they had been given in Christ? How does loving one another demonstrate that a person is walking in the Spirit (see verses 13–15)?

_____

_____

_____

_____

_____

_____

_____

GOING DEEPER

Paul was concerned the Galatians were choosing to put themselves under a "yoke of bondage" to the law. This yoke was heavy, burdensome, and also ineffective, for putting it on would never enable them to get where they wanted to go. But in the Gospel of Matthew, we find that Jesus offers His followers a different—and much better—kind of "yoke."

Jesus Gives True Rest (Matthew 11:25–30)

[25] At that time Jesus answered and said, "I thank You, Father, Lord of heaven and earth, that You have hidden these things from the wise and prudent and have revealed them to babes. [26] Even so, Father, for so it seemed good in Your sight. [27] All things have been delivered to Me by My Father, and no one knows the Son except the Father. Nor does anyone know the Father except the Son, and the one to whom the Son wills to reveal Him. [28] Come to Me, all you who labor and are heavy laden, and I will give you rest. [29] Take My yoke upon you and learn from Me, for I am gentle and lowly in heart, and you will find rest for your souls. [30] For My yoke is easy and My burden is light."

5. What invitation does Jesus offer to people who labor to fulfill the law and are heavy laden by its rules and restrictions (see verse 28)?

_____

_____

_____

_____

_____

_____

_____

6. How does Jesus describe His yoke? What happens to those who choose to take on His yoke instead of the yoke of the law (see verses 29–30)?

_____

_____

_____

_____

_____

_____

_____

Other writers of the Bible likewise point to this idea of taking on God's "yoke" and entering into His rest. In the following well-known psalm, King David draws on the metaphor of God being our Shepherd, leading us beside still waters, and restoring our souls. David's message is that God is with us even in the presence of our enemies . . . and that He will never fail us.

The Lord Is Our Shepherd (Psalm 23:1–6)

¹ The LORD is my shepherd;
I shall not want.

² He makes me to lie down in green pastures;
He leads me beside the still waters.
³ He restores my soul;
He leads me in the paths of righteousness
For His name's sake.

⁴ Yea, though I walk through the valley of the shadow of death,
I will fear no evil;
For You are with me;
Your rod and Your staff, they comfort me.
⁵ You prepare a table before me in the presence of my enemies;
You anoint my head with oil;
My cup runs over.

⁶ Surely goodness and mercy shall follow me
All the days of my life;
And I will dwell in the house of the Lᴏʀᴅ
Forever.

7. How does David describe the presence of God in his life? What does God do to provide rest and restoration for our souls (see verses 1–3)?

_____

_____

_____

_____

_____

_____

_____

_____

_____

8. How does God provide comfort even in the presence of our enemies? What promise do we have in this passage that God will always be with us (see verses 4–6)?

_____

_____

_____

_____

_____

_____

_____

REVIEWING THE STORY

Paul intensified his warnings to the Galatian believers about turning back to the law. He compared the law to a yoke of bondage. He warned that embracing the law would cause them to be estranged from Christ. He emphasized they would become responsible for fulfilling the *whole* law—not just parts of it. He also lamented the fact the Galatians had started so strong but had allowed false teachers to lead them away from the truth. He reminded them they had been called to liberty and to serve one another in love.

9. What happens when Christians attempt to be justified by the law (see Galatians 5:4)?

_____

_____

_____

_____

_____

_____

10. Paul states there is no difference in being circumcised or uncircumcised—in being a Jew or a Gentile—for all are one in Christ. What does matter in a person's life (see Galatians 5:6)?

_____

_____

_____

_____

_____

_____

_____

11. What warning does Paul issue about Christian liberty (see Galatians 5:13)?

_____

_____

_____

_____

_____

_____

12. How does Paul summarize the fulfillment of all the law (see Galatians 5:14)?

_____

_____

_____

_____

_____

_____

APPLYING THE MESSAGE

13. What circumstances make it especially difficult for you to stand fast when you face challenges in your walk with Christ?

_____

_____

_____

_____

_____

_____

_____

14. How can you demonstrate your Christian liberty today by loving your neighbor?

_____

_____

_____

_____

_____

_____

_____

REFLECTING ON THE MEANING

Paul has begun to bring his arguments in support of the gospel of grace to its natural conclusion. In this portion of his letter to the Galatians, he provides us with two key points that reveal what a Spirit-filled life looks like.

First, as Christians *we wait in hope*. Paul writes, "For we through the Spirit eagerly wait for the hope of righteousness by faith" (5:5). The law promises an immediate reward for living according to its rules. A person might revel in the fact that he has not murdered anyone or committed adultery or stolen any property. He could honestly brag that he has kept all of the feast days and honored the Sabbath and given his tithes.

But such conduct never provides a genuine reward, because it leaves that person feeling empty. At the core of his being, he knows it is not enough. And the longer he tries to live life by the law, the more he realizes how impossible it is to achieve any lasting peace. His reward is fleeting and it fades away. However, when we live by faith in Jesus Christ, the Holy Spirit comes to live within us—and He brings the lasting reward of hope and the assurance of righteousness in Christ. We have a hope in righteousness that is ours purely through faith.

Second, as Christians *we work in love*. Paul continues, "For in Christ Jesus neither circumcision nor uncircumcision avails anything, but faith working through love" (verse 6). Here again is the balance that Paul displays in his teaching. Yes, we are saved by grace and grace alone. Salvation is the same whether we are Jews (circumcision) or Gentiles (uncircumcision). But while salvation does not occur *by* good works, it is for the *purpose* of good works.

In many of his letters, Paul goes out of his way to teach the relationship between our faith and our works. In Ephesians 2:8–10 he writes, "For by grace you have been saved through faith, and that not of yourselves; it is the gift of God, not of works, lest anyone should boast. For we are His workmanship, created in Christ Jesus for good works, which God prepared beforehand that we should walk in them." We are saved not by works, but that we might do good works that God has prepared for us in His sovereign will.

Christianity is faith working through love, not the flesh working through self-effort. For believers in Jesus Christ, any good works they are a part of are the product of their faith and not a substitute for it. What really matters in the end is faith, hope, and love . . . for our faith as followers of Christ provides hope for each day and motivates us to serve others with love.

JOURNALING YOUR RESPONSE

In what area of your life today do you need to experience God's rest for your soul?

WALK IN THE SPIRIT

Galatians 5:16–26

GETTING STARTED

What are some particular character traits that you would like to possess in greater abundance?

SETTING THE STAGE

As we have seen, Paul's primary message in Galatians is that we no longer have to try to measure up to any unattainable standard on our own because Jesus Christ has already measured up to that standard on our behalf. However, as followers of Christ, it is not enough for us to just accept what He has done . . . and then go back to living as we did in our former lives. Now that we are in a right relationship with Him, we need to *live* like Him.

The apostle Paul summed up this concept in his letter to the Romans when he wrote, "Do not be conformed to this world, but be transformed by the renewing of your mind, that you may prove what is that good and acceptable and perfect will of God" (12:2). This is the challenge that Paul is posing to the believers in Galatia. While they are no longer being led by the standards of the law, the Lord is still leading them—though He is now doing it through the work of the Holy Spirit. The believers need to recognize this guidance in their lives, put their former sinful ways behind them, and walk in step with the Holy Spirit's direciton.

It is clear from Paul's words there *were* individuals in the Galatian churches who were gratitfying their own desires at the expense of others—and this was leading to strife. Paul's charge to them is to live as they were called to live—as children of God and children of the promise. The victory we desire to have will never come through struggling in our own power—it will only come through surrender to Christ and the Holy Spirit. And when we do, our lives will be marked not by the sins of the flesh, but by the fruit of the Spirit. All of this derives from salvation in Christ . . . and Christ alone!

EXPLORING THE TEXT

The Contrast Between the Spirit and the Flesh (Galatians 5:16–21)

> [16] I say then: Walk in the Spirit, and you shall not fulfill the lust of the flesh. [17] For the flesh lusts against the Spirit, and the Spirit against the flesh; and these are contrary to one another, so that you do not

do the things that you wish. [18] But if you are led by the Spirit, you are not under the law.

[19] Now the works of the flesh are evident, which are: adultery, fornication, uncleanness, lewdness, [20] idolatry, sorcery, hatred, contentions, jealousies, outbursts of wrath, selfish ambitions, dissensions, heresies, [21] envy, murders, drunkenness, revelries, and the like; of which I tell you beforehand, just as I also told you in time past, that those who practice such things will not inherit the kingdom of God.

1. What does it mean to "walk in the Spirit"? How does this help a person to not give in to the temptations of sin (see verses 16–18)?

2. What happens to people who practice "the works of the flesh" (see verses 19, 21)?

Walking in the Spirit (Galatians 5:22–26)

> [22] But the fruit of the Spirit is love, joy, peace, longsuffering, kindness, goodness, faithfulness, [23] gentleness, self-control. Against such there is no law. [24] And those who are Christ's have crucified the flesh with its passions and desires. [25] If we live in the Spirit, let us also walk in the Spirit. [26] Let us not become conceited, provoking one another, envying one another.

3. Paul describes these attributes in a Christian's life as "the fruit of the Spirit." Why do you think he uses this analogy? What does "the fruit of the Spirit" look like (see verses 22–23)?

_____

_____

_____

_____

_____

4. In what three things does Paul warn the Galatians not to engage as he wraps up his discussion of the fruit of the Spirit (see verse 26)?

_____

_____

_____

_____

_____

_____

_____

GOING DEEPER

Paul wanted the Galatians to refuse the shackles of bondage to the law and embrace the freedom they had received through faith in Christ. However, as we have seen, he was aware of his opponents' criticism that such a course would lead to an anything-goes approach to life. Paul wanted to be clear that when the Holy Spirit truly dwells in a person, it brings about a change in that person's thoughts, attitudes, and behaviors. In the following passage, he expounds on this point and shows us what walking in the light and in wisdom looks like.

Walk in Light (Ephesians 5:8–13)

[8] For you were once darkness, but now you are light in the Lord. Walk as children of light [9] (for the fruit of the Spirit is in all goodness, righteousness, and truth), [10] finding out what is acceptable to the Lord. [11] And have no fellowship with the unfruitful works of darkness, but rather expose them. [12] For it is shameful even to speak of those things which are done by them in secret. [13] But all things that are exposed are made manifest by the light, for whatever makes manifest is light.

5. Paul notes the believers were in spiritual darkness before they came into the light of Christ. What traits appear when someone is truly walking in the light (see verses 8–10)?

6. What does Paul urge his readers to do as it relates to the works of darkness? How does the light of Christ serve to expose such works (see verses 11–13)?

_____

_____

_____

_____

_____

_____

Walk in Wisdom (Ephesians 5:15–21)

¹⁵ See then that you walk circumspectly, not as fools but as wise, ¹⁶ redeeming the time, because the days are evil.

¹⁷ Therefore do not be unwise, but understand what the will of the Lord is. ¹⁸ And do not be drunk with wine, in which is dissipation; but be filled with the Spirit, ¹⁹ speaking to one another in psalms and hymns and spiritual songs, singing and making melody in your heart to the Lord, ²⁰ giving thanks always for all things to God the Father in the name of our Lord Jesus Christ, ²¹ submitting to one another in the fear of God.

7. What does it mean to "walk circumspectly"? Why is it critical for believers in Christ to walk in wisdom (see verses 15–16)?

_____

_____

_____

_____

_____

8. What are some practices that Paul notes as being unwise for a believer in Christ to do? What are some wise practices that a believer should do (see verses 17–21)?

_____

_____

_____

_____

_____

REVIEWING THE STORY

Paul warned the Galatians about the battle they were engaged in between the flesh and the Spirit. He reminded them again that if they were led by the Spirit, they were not under the law—and their lives should reflect the light of Christ within them. According to Paul, the best way to avoid the sins of the flesh is to walk in the Spirit. The Galatians were to allow the fruit of the Spirit to grow within them—traits such as love, joy, peace, long-suffering, kindness, goodness, faithfulness, gentleness, and self-control. As they celebrated the Spirit's work in their lives, they should guard against becoming conceited, provoking one another, and envying one another.

9. How do believers avoid giving in to the lust of the flesh (see Galatians 5:16)?

_____

_____

_____

_____

_____

10. What is the unfortunate result of the constant battle between the flesh and the Spirit (see Galatians 5:17)?

_____

_____

_____

_____

11. What point does Paul make about the nine qualities that he lists as the fruit of the Spirit (see Galatians 5:23)?

_____

_____

_____

12. If we live in the Spirit, what else should we do (Galatians 5:25)?

_____

_____

_____

_____

APPLYING THE MESSAGE

13. Which of the items Paul lists as the works of the flesh present a struggle for you? Why?

_____

_____

_____

_____

_____

14. Which of the qualities Paul lists as the fruit of the Spirit do you most want to incorporate into your life? How can you do so?

_____

_____

_____

_____

_____

_____

REFLECTING ON THE MEANING

If you are a Christian, the Holy Spirit is leading you. When you give your life to Christ, you receive God's Spirit to serve as your dynamic GPS system. But will you follow His directions?

Unlike actual GPS systems, the Holy Spirit never makes a mistake. Of course, this does not mean His directions are always easy to follow. Sometimes, in fact, they are extremely difficult to obey. Jesus was clear that following Him would not always be easy—and it would require much from us. "If anyone comes to Me and does not hate his father and mother, wife and children, brothers and sisters, yes, and his own life also, he cannot be My disciple. And whoever does not bear his cross and come after Me cannot be My disciple" (Luke 14:26–27). But ignoring the Holy Spirit's leading only brings trouble and negative consequences in our lives.

Walking in the Spirit means listening to the Holy Spirit—in the Word of God or in prayer—and following His directions. As we do this, the Holy Spirit will lead us, regardless of whether we follow or not. He will point us in the right direction, but He will not coerce us or go against our will. The Holy Spirit is not _driving_ us forward—He is _leading_ us forward.

And where is the Holy Spirit leading us? He wants to make us like Jesus. That is His purpose. If we will give Him free reign, the Holy Spirit will develop in us the Christlike attributes of Jesus. And in so doing, the temptations of the flesh will fade from our lives.

Journaling Your Response

What is one action you sense the Holy Spirit is leading you to do right now?

LESSON *eleven*

BEARING EACH OTHER'S BURDENS

Galatians 6:1–10

GETTING STARTED

What is the most difficult thing about confronting someone who is doing something wrong?

_____

_____

_____

_____

_____

_____

_____

_____

_____

_____

_____

_____

_____

_____

_____

SETTING THE STAGE

Every news cycle seems to bring with it an account of a moral failure on the part of a nationally known and respected leader. Sometimes it involves a political figure—often one who stood for the strongest principles but then failed to live by them. Sometimes, it involves a business figure—one who took a less-than-legal shortcut in an effort to get ahead. Whatever the reason for the failure—whether lust, greed, or something else—we can find ourselves discouraged when someone we respected and trusted proved themselves to be unworthy of our respect and trust.

Spiritual leaders aren't immune to such stunning falls from grace. It has been said that one of the worst things that ever happens to pastors is they stand on a platform above everybody else. This could lead to them thinking they live in a world that is above everybody else's world. They convince themselves they don't have to live by the same rules that other people live by. How often does that scenario play out in life? The people who are the most critical of others often end up stumbling themselves.

In this section of Galatians, Paul warns us about the danger of pride and shows us the proper way to restore a fallen brother or sister. Interestingly, Paul does not have anything to say to the *individual* who is overtaken by sin. Instead, he focuses on the humility of the *restorer*.

EXPLORING THE TEXT

Bear and Share Burdens (Galatians 6:1–5)

¹ Brethren, if a man is overtaken in any trespass, you who are spiritual restore such a one in a spirit of gentleness, considering yourself lest you also be tempted. ² Bear one another's burdens, and so fulfill the law of Christ. ³ For if anyone thinks himself to be something, when he is nothing, he deceives himself. ⁴ But let each one examine his own work, and then he will have rejoicing in himself alone, and not in another. ⁵ For each one shall bear his own load.

1. What is the responsibility of spiritually mature believers when someone is "overtaken in any trespass"? (verse 1)?

_____

_____

_____

_____

_____

2. Jesus said the greatest commandments were to "love the LORD your God with all your heart" and to "love your neighbor as yourself" (Matthew 22:37, 39). How does bearing one another's burdens fulfill "the law of Christ" (see Galatians 6:2)?

_____

_____

_____

_____

_____

_____

Be Generous and Do Good (Galatians 6:6–10)

⁶ Let him who is taught the word share in all good things with him who teaches.

⁷ Do not be deceived, God is not mocked; for whatever a man sows, that he will also reap. ⁸ For he who sows to his flesh will of the flesh reap corruption, but he who sows to the Spirit will of the Spirit reap everlasting life. ⁹ And let us not grow weary while doing good, for in due season we shall reap if we do not lose heart. ¹⁰ Therefore, as we have opportunity, let us do good to all, especially to those who are of the household of faith.

3. What will happen to a person who sows in the flesh? What happens to the person who sows to the Spirit (see verse 8)?

_____

_____

_____

_____

_____

4. What promise does Paul give to those who have done good but not yet seen the results of their labor (see verses 9–10)?

_____

_____

_____

_____

GOING DEEPER

The term _admonish_ in the Bible means "to warn or notify of a fault, to reprove gently," and "to strongly encourage another to take a specific action." For the apostle Paul, the act of admonishing is always done out of a spirit of love and concern for the other person—and it is done kindly and gently. In the following passage, Paul instructs another congregation on the same issue.

Character of the New Man (Colossians 3:12–17)

12 Therefore, as the elect of God, holy and beloved, put on tender mercies, kindness, humility, meekness, longsuffering; 13 bearing with one another, and forgiving one another, if anyone has a complaint against another; even as Christ forgave you, so you also must do.

[14] But above all these things put on love, which is the bond of perfection. [15] And let the peace of God rule in your hearts, to which also you were called in one body; and be thankful. [16] Let the word of Christ dwell in you richly in all wisdom, teaching and admonishing one another in psalms and hymns and spiritual songs, singing with grace in your hearts to the Lord. [17] And whatever you do in word or deed, do all in the name of the Lord Jesus, giving thanks to God the Father through Him.

---

5. How does Paul instruct believers in Christ—whom he calls the "elect of God"—to treat one another (see verses 12–15)?

_____

_____

_____

_____

_____

6. How does Paul instruct the believers to admonish one another (see verses 16–17)?

_____

_____

_____

_____

_____

Of course, receiving admonishment is never an easy or enjoyable process. We do not like to have our mistakes and errors called out—but we need to recognize God will use our brothers and sisters in Christ to lead us back to the way that He has set for us. In the following passage, the author of Hebrews comments on this type of discipline from the Lord.

The Discipline of God (Hebrews 12:7–11)

7 If you endure chastening, God deals with you as with sons; for what son is there whom a father does not chasten? 8 But if you are without chastening, of which all have become partakers, then you are illegitimate and not sons. 9 Furthermore, we have had human fathers who corrected us, and we paid them respect. Shall we not much more readily be in subjection to the Father of spirits and live? 10 For they indeed for a few days chastened us as seemed best to them, but He for our profit, that we may be partakers of His holiness. 11 Now no chastening seems to be joyful for the present, but painful; nevertheless, afterward it yields the peaceable fruit of righteousness to those who have been trained by it.

7. Why does God discipline us (see verses 7)? Why should we be concerned if discipline is not a part of our lives (see verse 8)?

_____

_____

_____

_____

8. No chastening or discipline seems pleasant at the time. But what does it yield in our lives (see verse 11)?

_____

_____

_____

_____

REVIEWING THE STORY

Paul emphasized to the Galatians that they had a responsibility to one another. If one of them fell into sin, the others were to restore that person with a spirit of gentleness and humility. The Lord intends for us to bear one another's burdens. Paul warned the Galatians their actions had consequences. Those who sow corruption reap corruption. But those who "sow to the Spirit will of the Spirit reap" (Galatians 6:8).

9. What must spiritually mature believers guard against as they help restore someone who is caught up in sin (see Galatians 6:1)?

_____

_____

_____

_____

10. Paul indicates pride can keep us from sacrificial service to another (see Galatians 6:3). Is there an area in your life where this is the case?

_____

_____

_____

_____

11. According to Paul, what is the ideal relationship between a student of God's Word and a teacher of God's Word (see Galatians 6:6)?

_____

_____

_____

_____

12. Who should be the special focus of believers' goodwill (see Galatians 6:10)?

APPLYING THE MESSAGE

13. What did you do the last time you learned a fellow believer was struggling with a moral failure—or just struggling with his or her Christian faith?

14. What lessons did you learn from the experience that will help you the next time a situation like that arises?

REFLECTING ON THE MEANING

Throughout history, whenever the story of the prodigal son has been told, it usually has gone like this: the young man leaves home and goes to the far country and loses everything. He ends up slopping the pigs, and it is in the pigsty that he realizes that all he's got left in the world is at home. Many people say that right there in the middle of the pigsty, he was saved. He came to himself and he went home.

But that is not what happened. He just had a moment of rationality: "But when he came to himself, he said, 'How many of my father's hired servants have bread enough and to spare, and I perish with hunger! I will arise and go to my father, and will say to him, "Father, I have sinned against heaven and before you, and I am no longer worthy to be called your son"'" (Luke 15:17–19). The son looked around at the pigs and remembered his home. That's all he wanted in that moment. He wasn't saved in the far country. No, no, no! The Bible says he *came home* and got to the edge of the village that he had grown up in. And all this time, his father had been standing on a high place waiting and watching for him.

Remember that on his way back, the prodigal had concocted a speech that he was going to give to try to get back into the good graces of his father. Perhaps his father would let him be a servant. But as he drew near, his father saw him on the horizon. And that old man—dressed in his Jewish garb—pulled that robe up around his legs and ran like a fool to where his son was. Before the son could ever say one word, his father wrapped him in his arms and began to kiss his son again and again. It was the love of the father welcoming his boy back home that was the moment of his salvation.

The Bible says that no one seeks God. God is the Seeker. So when it comes to helping brothers or sisters who have fallen into sin, we are to be like our God. We are to rush to those people with open arms, embrace them, and tell them of our love—then we are to help them get their lives back in order. We are to pick up their burden, carry it, and bring them back home. That is the heart of God. And as followers of Jesus, that should be our heart as well.

Journaling Your Response

How can you take the first step in reaching out to someone who is struggling spiritually?

GRACE GETS THE LAST WORD

Galatians 6:11–18

GETTING STARTED

How would you describe the power of God's grace in your life?

_____

_____

_____

_____

_____

_____

_____

_____

_____

_____

_____

_____

_____

_____

_____

_____

_____

SETTING THE STAGE

Throughout this letter, Paul has defended the Galatian believers and himself from the attacks of the Judaizers and false prophets. Most importantly, he has championed and articulated the gospel of grace with authority and power. As he concludes this great letter, Paul bursts forth once more with a magnificent appeal to the supremacy of grace and salvation by faith in Christ alone. If we can understand these verses, we will have understood the entire book.

Paul has faithfully championed the cause of grace and freedom throughout this entire letter, and now he concludes with some final passionate words. His final word in Galatians is the same as his first word—it is the word *grace* (see Galatians 1:3 and 6:18). The false teachers had nothing to offer but the law and the demands that went with it. But Paul has consistently offered the Galatians grace.

Remember that Paul was so angry at the Galatians that he initially called them "foolish." But through the course of the letter he has come a long way in appreciating the growth of this church. And so he concludes by calling them "brethren" and saying "Amen," a reminder of his love for them and his desire to pray for them.

EXPLORING THE TEXT

Glory Only in the Cross (Galatians 6:11–15)

11 See with what large letters I have written to you with my own hand! 12 As many as desire to make a good showing in the flesh, these would compel you to be circumcised, only that they may not suffer persecution for the cross of Christ. 13 For not even those who are circumcised keep the law, but they desire to have you circumcised that they may boast in your flesh. 14 But God forbid that I should boast except in the cross of our Lord Jesus Christ, by whom the world has been crucified to me, and I to the world. 15 For in Christ

Jesus neither circumcision nor uncircumcision avails anything, but a new creation.

_____

1. Paul would evidently dictate his letters to a scribe who recorded his words (see, for example, Romans 16:22). Why do you think Paul mentions that he has written this portion of the letter (see Galatians 6:11)? What purpose would this serve?

_____

_____

_____

_____

_____

_____

_____

_____

2. What "secret" does Paul reveal about the church leaders from Jerusalem who were pressuring the Galatian believers to be circumcised (see verse 13)?

_____

_____

_____

_____

_____

_____

_____

_____

lessing and a Plea (Galatians 6:16–18)

16 And as many as walk according to this rule, peace and mercy be upon them, and upon the Israel of God.

17 From now on let no one trouble me, for I bear in my body the marks of the Lord Jesus.

18 Brethren, the grace of our Lord Jesus Christ be with your spirit. Amen.

---

3. Paul prays for peace for those who walk by the rule—those who live by grace. Why is peace a result of basing your relationship with God on grace instead of works?

_____

_____

_____

_____

_____

4. Paul mentions he has been scarred for the cause of Christ (see verse 17). Why do you think he calls out this fact at the end of his letter?

_____

_____

_____

_____

_____

_____

_____

GOING DEEPER

As a mentor to young Christians, Paul frequently had to deliver difficult truths to people who did not want to hear them. Truth-telling was risky, but he believed in the message of grace to the extent he was willing to suffer for it. He even carried in his own body "the marks of the Lord Jesus." In the passages below, Paul detailed many of the ordeals and trials he endured for the sake of the gospel.

Cast Down but Unconquered (2 Corinthians 4:7–12)

7 But we have this treasure in earthen vessels, that the excellence of the power may be of God and not of us. 8 We are hard-pressed on every side, yet not crushed; we are perplexed, but not in despair; 9 persecuted, but not forsaken; struck down, but not destroyed— 10 always carrying about in the body the dying of the Lord Jesus, that the life of Jesus also may be manifested in our body. 11 For we who live are always delivered to death for Jesus' sake, that the life of Jesus also may be manifested in our mortal flesh. 12 So then death is working in us, but life in you.

5. In this passage, Paul stresses it is the *message* of the gospel that is the treasure—not the *bearers* of that gospel. What had the power of the gospel enabled Paul to endure? How had the power of that gospel motivated him to persevere (see verses 7–10)?

_____

_____

_____

_____

_____

_____

. How did Paul defend his authority to preach the gospel? In what
does he say he will be bold (see verses 21–23)?

_____

_____

_____

_____

Suffering for Christ (2 Corinthians 11:24–31)

24 From the Jews five times I received forty stripes minus one. 25 Three
times I was beaten with rods; once I was stoned; three times I was
shipwrecked; a night and a day I have been in the deep; 26 in journeys
often, in perils of waters, in perils of robbers, in perils of my own
countrymen, in perils of the Gentiles, in perils in the city, in perils in
the wilderness, in perils in the sea, in perils among false brethren;
27 in weariness and toil, in sleeplessness often, in hunger and thirst,
in fastings often, in cold and nakedness—28 besides the other things,
what comes upon me daily: my deep concern for all the churches.
29 Who is weak, and I am not weak? Who is made to stumble, and I
do not burn with indignation?

30 If I must boast, I will boast in the things which concern my
infirmity. 31 The God and Father of our Lord Jesus Christ, who is
blessed forever, knows that I am not lying.

7. What other kinds of suffering had Paul endured to preach the gospel
(see verses 24–27)?

_____

_____

_____

_____

8. Why do you think Paul was willing to endure all these various tria.
(see verse 28)?

_____

_____

_____

_____

REVIEWING THE STORY

Paul called special attention to this final section of this letter by highlight-
ing the fact that he was writing it in his own hand. (The rest of the letter
had been dictated to a secretary.) He reminded his readers of the hypocrisy
of the false teachers. They were demanding the Galatians keep the law
even though they were not keeping it themselves. Paul concluded by issuing
a prayer of blessing for all who would remain committed to walking in
grace—asking God to grant His peace and mercy to them.

9. What was the only boasting that was acceptable to the apostle Paul
(see Galatians 6:14)?

_____

_____

_____

_____

10. What does Christ Jesus offer that is superior to circumcision, which
focuses on only one part of the body (see Galatians 6:15)?

_____

_____

_____

_____

11. What blessings did Paul offer for those who walk according to faith (see Galatians 6:16)?

_____

_____

_____

_____

_____

_____

12. What word did Paul use in his closing to indicate his true feelings about the Galatians (see Galatians 6:18)? Why is this significant?

_____

_____

_____

_____

_____

_____

APPLYING THE MESSAGE

13. Why is it often so difficult for people to accept God's grace?

_____

_____

_____

_____

_____

14. What "marks"—physical, emotional, relational, spiritual—do you bear as a result of standing firm in your Christian faith?

_____

_____

_____

_____

_____

_____

_____

REFLECTING ON THE MEANING

Paul's final sentence of the letter of Galatians reads, "Brethren, the grace of our Lord Jesus Christ be with your spirit. Amen" (6:18). If you study the letters of Paul, you will see he actually ended many of them with grace. Why? Because for Paul, it was the grace of God that took him from being a persecutor of the church and turned him into a preacher and leader of the Church of Jesus Christ. Whether we are judges or thieves, saints or sinners, Jews or Gentiles, we all stand in absolute need of the grace of God. There is nothing that any of us can do to earn what God wants to give us as a gift.

Some of us may consider ourselves to be at the bottom of the totem pole. Others may consider themselves to be at the top. But it makes no difference at all. When God sees us, He sees us all together as sinners who need to be saved. The only way He saves anyone—no matter how good or bad we are—is through the wonderful grace that He has provided.

Let's remember that we have not been called to fix the world. Instead, we have been called to share the gospel of Jesus Christ and to bring as many to heaven with us as we can through the message of God's free grace. May God help us to do that as never before, and let us never forget the importance of this book. Hallelujah!

JOURNALING YOUR RESPONSE

How can you make sure that grace gets the last word in your life?

LEADER'S GUIDE

Thank you for choosing to lead your group through this study from Dr. David Jeremiah on *The Letter to the Galatians*. Being a group leader has its own rewards, and it is our prayer that your walk with the Lord will deepen through this experience. During the twelve lessons in this study, you and your group will read selected passages from Galatians, explore key themes in the letter based on teachings from Dr. Jeremiah, and review questions that will encourage group discussion. There are multiple components in this section that can help you structure your lessons and discussion time, so please be sure to read and consider each one.

BEFORE YOU BEGIN

Before your first meeting, make sure you and your group are well-versed with the content of the lesson. Group members should have their own copy of *The Letter to the Galatians* study guide prior to the first meeting so they can follow along and record their answers, thoughts, and insights. After the first week, you may wish to assign the study guide lesson as homework prior to the group meeting and then use the meeting time to discuss the content in the lesson.

To ensure everyone has a chance to participate in the discussion, the ideal size for a group is around eight to ten people. If there are more than ten people, break up the bigger group into smaller subgroups. Make sure the members are committed to participating each week, as this will help create stability and help you better prepare the structure of the meeting.

At the beginning of each week's study, start with the opening Getting Started question to introduce the topic you will be discussing.

The members should answer briefly, as the goal is just for them to have an idea of the subject in their minds as you go over the lesson. This will allow the members to become engaged and ready to interact with the rest of the group.

After reviewing the lesson, try to initiate a free-flowing discussion. Invite group members to bring questions and insights they may have discovered to the next meeting, especially if they were unsure of the meaning of some parts of the lesson. Be prepared to discuss how biblical truth applies to the world we live in today.

WEEKLY PREPARATION

As the group leader, here are a few things you can do to prepare for each meeting:

- *Be thoroughly familiar with the material in the lesson*. Make sure that you understand the content of each lesson so you know how to structure the group time and are prepared to lead the group discussion.

- *Decide, ahead of time, which questions you want to discuss*. Depending on how much time you have each week, you may not be able to reflect on every question. Select specific questions that you feel will evoke the best discussion.

- *Take prayer requests*. At the end of your discussion, take prayer requests from your group members and then pray for one another.

STRUCTURING THE DISCUSSION TIME

There are several ways to structure the duration of the study. You can choose to cover each lesson individually, for a total of twelve weeks of group meetings, or you can combine two lessons together per week, for a total of six weeks of group meetings. The following charts illustrate these options:

TWELVE-WEEK FORMAT

Week	Lessons Covered	Reading
1	The One True Gospel	*Galatians 1:1–10*
2	Grace Under Fire	*Galatians 1:11–24*
3	The Freedom Fighter	*Galatians 2:1–10*
4	Confrontation Over the Gospel	*Galatians 2:11–21*
5	Bewitched	*Galatians 3:1–14*
6	The Law and the Promise	*Galatians 3:15–29*
7	Time to Grow Up	*Galatians 4:1–20*
8	A Tale of Two Sons	*Galatians 4:21–31*
9	The Law of Liberty	*Galatians 5:1–15*
10	Walk in the Spirit	*Galatians 5:16–26*
11	Bearing Each Other's Burdens	*Galatians 6:1–10*
12	Grace Gets the Last Word	*Galatians 6:11–18*

SIX-WEEK FORMAT

Week	Lessons Covered	Reading
1	The One True Gospel / Grace Under Fire	*Galatians 1:1–24*
2	The Freedom Fighter / Confrontation Over the Gospel	*Galatians 2:1–21*
3	Bewitched / The Law and the Promise	*Galatians 3:1–29*
4	Time to Grow Up / A Tale of Two Sons	*Galatians 4:1–31*
5	The Law of Liberty / Walk in the Spirit	*Galatians 5:1–26*
6	Bearing Each Other's Burdens / Grace Gets the Last Word	*Galatians 6:1–18*

In regard to organizing your time when planning your group Bible study, the following two schedules, for sixty minutes and ninety minutes, can give you a structure for the lesson:

Section	60 Minutes	90 Minutes
Welcome: Members arrive and get settled	5 minutes	10 minutes
Getting Started Question: Prepares the group for interacting with one another	10 minutes	10 minutes
Message: Review the lesson	15 minutes	25 minutes
Discussion: Discuss questions in the lesson	25 minutes	35 minutes
Review and Prayer: Review the key points of the lesson and have a closing time of prayer	5 minutes	10 minutes

As the group leader, it is up to you to keep track of the time and keep things moving according to your schedule. If your group is having a good discussion, don't feel the need to stop and move on to the next question. Remember, the purpose is to pull together ideas and share unique insights on the lesson. Encourage everyone to participate, but don't be concerned if certain group members are more quiet. They may just be internally reflecting on the questions and need time to process their ideas before they can share them.

GROUP DYNAMICS

Leading a group study can be a rewarding experience for you and your group members—but that doesn't mean there won't be challenges. Certain members may feel uncomfortable discussing topics that they consider very personal and might be afraid of being called on. Some members might have disagreements on specific issues. To help prevent these scenarios, consider the following ground rules:

- If someone has a question that may seem off topic, suggest that it is discussed at another time, or ask the group if they are okay with addressing that topic.

- If someone asks a question you don't know the answer to, confess that you don't know and move on. If you feel comfortable, invite other group members to give their opinions or share their comments based on personal experience.
- If you feel like a couple of people are talking much more than others, direct questions to people who may not have shared yet. You could even ask the more dominating members to help draw out the quiet ones.
- When there is a disagreement, encourage the group members to process the matter in love. Invite members from opposing sides to evaluate their opinions and consider the ideas of the other members. Lead the group through Scripture that addresses the topic, and look for common ground.

When issues arise, encourage your group to think of Scripture: "Love one another" (John 13:34), "If it is possible, as much as it depends on you, live peaceably with all men" (Romans 12:18), and, "Be swift to hear, slow to speak, slow to wrath" (James 1:19).

ABOUT
Dr. David Jeremiah and Turning Point

Dr. David Jeremiah is the founder of Turning Point, a ministry committed to providing Christians with sound Bible teaching relevant to today's changing times through radio and television broadcasts, audio series, books, and live events. Dr. Jeremiah's teaching on topics such as family, prayer, worship, angels, and biblical prophecy forms the foundation of Turning Point.

David and his wife, Donna, reside in El Cajon, California, where he serves as the senior pastor of Shadow Mountain Community Church. David and Donna have four children and twelve grandchildren.

In 1982, Dr. Jeremiah brought the same solid teaching to San Diego television that he shares weekly with his congregation. Shortly thereafter, Turning Point expanded its ministry to radio. Dr. Jeremiah's inspiring messages can now be heard worldwide on radio, television, and the internet.

Because Dr. Jeremiah desires to know his listening audience, he travels nationwide holding ministry rallies and spiritual enrichment conferences that touch the hearts and lives of many people. According to Dr. Jeremiah, "At some point in time, everyone reaches a turning point; and for every person, that moment is unique, an experience to hold onto forever. There's so much changing in today's world that sometimes it's difficult to choose the right path. Turning Point offers people an understanding of God's Word and seeks to make a difference in their lives."

Dr. Jeremiah has authored numerous books, including *Escape the Coming Night* (Revelation), *The Handwriting on the Wall* (Daniel), *Overcoming Loneliness, Prayer—The Great Adventure, God in You* (Holy Spirit), *When*

Your World Falls Apart, Slaying the Giants in Your Life, My Heart's Desire, Hope for Today, Captured by Grace, Signs of Life, What in the World Is Going On?, The Coming Economic Armageddon, I Never Thought I'd See the Day!, God Loves You: He Always Has—He Always Will, Agents of the Apocalypse, Agents of Babylon, Revealing the Mysteries of Heaven, People Are Asking . . . Is This the End?, A Life Beyond Amazing, Overcomer, and *The Book of Signs.*

New Bible Study Series from Dr. David Jeremiah

The Jeremiah Bible Study Series captures Dr. David Jeremiah's forty-plus years of commitment to teaching the whole Word of God. Each volume contains twelve lessons for individuals and groups to explore what the Bible says, what it meant to the people at the time it was written, and what it means to us today. Out of his lifelong ministry of *delivering the unchanging Word of God to an ever-changing world*, Dr. Jeremiah has written this Bible-strong study series focused not on causes, current events, or politics, but on the solid truth of Scripture.

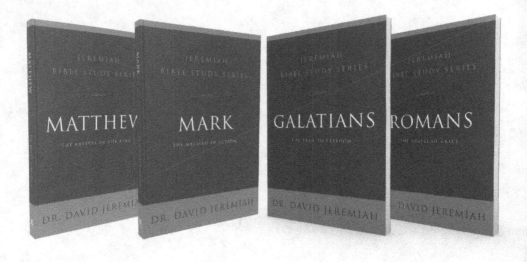

9780310091493	Matthew	9780310091554	John
9780310091516	Mark	9780310091608	Acts
9780310091530	Luke	9780310091622	Romans

9780310091646	1 Corinthians
9780310097488	2 Corinthians
9780310091660	Galatians

Available now at your favorite bookstore.
More volumes coming soon.

Harper*Christian* Resources